MONETARY THEORY AND THE
TRADE CYCLE

MONETARY THEORY

AND THE

TRADE CYCLE

by

FRIEDRICH A. HAYEK

**Tooke Professor of Economic Science and Statistics
in the University of London**

Translated from the German
by
N. KALDOR AND H. M. CROOME

AUGUSTUS M. KELLEY • PUBLISHERS

CLIFTON *1975*

First Published 1933

Reprinted 1966 and 1975 by

Augustus M. Kelley Publishers

Clifton New Jersey 07012

Library of Congress Cataloged.
The original printing of this title as follows:

Hayek, Friedrich August von, 1899–
 Monetary theory and the trade cycle, by Friedrich A.
Hayek. Translated from the German by N. Kaldor and
H. M. Croome. New York, A. M. Kelley, 1966.

 244 p. 21 cm. (Reprints of economic classics)

 Translation of Geldtheorie und Konjunkturtheorie.
 Reprint of the 1933 ed.
 Bibliographical footnotes.

 1. Business cycles. 2. Money. 3. Prices. 4. Quantity theory of
money. i. Title.

HB3711.H36 1966   338.54   66–22629
ISBN 0–678–00176–6

HB
3711
·H36
1975

PRINTED IN THE UNITED STATES OF AMERICA
by SENTRY PRESS, NEW YORK, N. Y. 10013
Bound by A. HOROWITZ & SON, CLIFTON, N. J.

INTRODUCTION TO THE SERIES

THE science of Economics, like all other branches of knowledge, recognizes no limitation by national boundaries. Contiguity of residence may give a certain unity to the speculation of particular groups of economists, a tradition of good teaching may give a presumption of excellence to the products of particular seminars; and in this sense it is not foolish to speak of local schools of economic thought, or to attach geographical labels to particular theories. But to speak of Economics, as distinct from economists, in terms of national or municipal classifications, to distinguish an English Economics from a Continental Economics, and so on, has no more sense than to speak of English Arithmetic. The criteria of scientific validity take no account of origins, and the economist who refused to avail himself of a particular set of propositions because they were foreign would be acting no less unscientifically than the chemist or physicist who acted on

5

similar principles. It has been well said that there are only two kinds of Economics — good Economics and bad Economics. All other classifications are misleading.

Unfortunately, the economist, far more than the practitioner of the natural sciences, is victim to the curse of Babel. The chemist and the physicist — dealing as they do with tangible and quantitative relations between easily definable things — can converse in what to all intents and purposes is an international language. A very modest linguistic equipment is sufficient to enable one to follow all the chief contributions in such branches of science. In Economics this is not so. The complicated social relationships which are its chief preoccupation lend themselves much less to merely symbolic analysis. No doubt, even here, mathematical methods can be of considerable use both in assisting thought and in securing complete precision. But the description of what the symbols represent, the delimitation and interpretation of concepts, these are matters which, in the social sciences, require a wealth of qualitative terminology and a subtlety of expression calculated to strain to the full the resources of any language. Small wonder, then, that the professional economist, with limited time and limited powers at his disposal, will often conclude that depth is to be preferred to breadth and that a more intensive exploitation of the resources available to him in his own language is likely to yield more than the attempt to assimilate material only available in foreign tongues. Small wonder too that, in consequence of these conditions, there is probably more overlapping and wasteful duplication of effort in Economics than in any other branch of scientific knowledge. I know of no natural science in which it would be possible for a man to devote years to the discovery of propositions which are already commonplaces in language areas other than his own. It is notorious that in Economics this frequently happens.

It follows, therefore, that, in Economics, even more than elsewhere, there is an urgent need for a continuous series of translations which shall make available to economists in different countries the results of investigations in languages other than their own. In England before the war this need was beginning to be met. The Bruce translation of Pantaleoni, the Wotzel translation of Pierson, the Smart translations of Böhm-Bawerk, are examples of work of a high order of scholarship and literary excellence which kept us in touch with the best products of contemporary thought abroad. But the war (which upset so many good things) interrupted this process of internationalization, and since the war it has not been completely resumed. This series is an attempt to make good the gap — to make available to English and American readers the chief recent contributions in foreign languages to the advancement of Economic Science.

It is unnecessary to introduce at length the author of the present volume, Professor von Hayek, until recently Director of the Austrian Institut für Konjunkturforschung, now Tooke Professor of Economic Science and Statistics in the University of London. Professor Hayek's *Prices and Production*, and his various contributions to *Economica* and the *Economic Journal* will already have made him familiar to most English readers interested in recent developments in the theory of money and credit. The present volume, *Monetary Theory and the Trade Cycle*, is a translation of a work which was published in Austria before *Prices and Production*, and which deals with the problem of trade fluctuation from a more general point of view. The preface makes clear the precise relationship between this work and the author's other investigations in the same field.

LIONEL ROBBINS

The London School of Economics
September 1932

CONTENTS

ANALYSIS OF CONTENTS

ANALYSIS OF CONTENTS

13

PREFACE

THE German essay*, of which the following is a translation, represents an expanded version of a paper† prepared for the meeting of the *Verein für Sozialpolitik*,‡ held in Zürich in September 1928, and of some remarks contributed to the discussion at that meeting. Although, in revising the translation, I have made numerous minor alterations and additions (mainly confined to the footnotes), the general course of the argument has been left unchanged. The book, therefore, still shows signs of the particular aim with which it was written. In submitting it to a public different from that for which it was originally intended, a few words of explanation are, perhaps, required.

---

* *Geldtheorie und Konjunkturtheorie* (Beitrage zur Konjunkturforschung, herausgegeben vom Österreichisches Institut für Konjunkturforschung, No. 1). Vienna 1929.

† *Einige Bemerkungen über das Verhältnis der Geldtheorie zur Konjunkturtheorie* in vol. 173, part 2 of the 'Schriften des Vereins fur Sozialpolitik,' München 1928.

‡ *Schriften des Vereins für Sozialpolitik*, vol. 175, pp. 369–374, München 1928.

PREFACE

In Germany, somewhat in contrast to the situation in English-speaking countries, monetary explanations of the Trade Cycle were always, or at least until quite recently, regarded with some mistrust. One of the aims of this study — one on which an English reader may feel that I have wasted unnecessary energy — was to justify the monetary approach to these problems. But I hope that this more explicit statement of the role of the monetary factor will not be found quite useless, for it is not only a justification of the monetary approach but also a refutation of some over-simplified monetary explanations which are widely accepted. In order to save the sound elements in the monetary theories of the Trade Cycle, I had to attempt, in particular, to refute certain theories which have led to the belief that, by stabilizing the general price level, all the disturbing monetary causes would be eliminated. Although, since this book was written, this belief has been somewhat rudely shaken by the crisis of 1929, I hope that a systematic examination of its foundations will still be found useful. The critique of the programme of the 'stabilizers', which is in many ways the central theme of this book, has now occupied me for many years, and since I deal here only with some special problems which have grown mainly out of these studies, I may perhaps be permitted to refer below to other publications, in which I have partly dealt with certain further theoretical problems and partly attempted to use these considerations for the elucidation of contemporary phenomena.* In particular, my *Prices and Production*, originally published in England, should be considered as an essential complement to the present publication. While I have here emphasized the *monetary causes* which *start* the cyclical fluctuations, I have, in that later publication, concentrated on the *successive changes in the real structure of production*, which *constitute* those fluctuations. This essential complement of my theory seems to me to be the

---

* *Die Währungspolitik der Vereinigten Staaten seit der Uberwindung der Krise von* 1920, Zeitschrift für Volkswirtschaft und Sozialpolitik, N.F., vol. v, 1925. *Das intertemporale Gleichgewichtssystem der Preise und die Bewegungen des Geldwertes*, 'Weltwirtschaftliches Archiv,' vol. 28, 1928, *The 'Paradox' of Saving*, 'Economica' No. 32, May 1931. *Prices and Production*, London, 1931. *Reflections on the Pure Theory of Money of Mr. J. M. Keynes*, 'Economica' Nos. 33–35, 1931–32. *Das Schicksal der Goldwährung*, Der Deutsche Volkswirt, 1932. *Kapitalaufzehrung*, 'Weltwirtschaftliches Archiv,' vol. 36, 1932.

more important since, in consequence of actual economic developments, the over-simplified monetary explanations have gained undeserved prominence in recent times. And since, in all my English publications, I have purposely refrained from combining purely theoretical considerations with discussions of current events, it may be useful to add here one or two remarks on the bearing of those considerations on the problems of to-day.

It is a curious fact that the general disinclination to explain the past boom by monetary factors has been quickly replaced by an even greater readiness to hold the present working of our monetary organization exclusively responsible for our present plight. And the same stabilizers who believed that nothing was wrong with the boom and that it might last indefinitely because prices did not rise, now believe that everything could be set right again if only we would use the weapons of monetary policy to prevent prices from falling. The same superficial view which sees no other harmful effect of a credit expansion but the rise of the price level, now believes that our only difficulty is a fall in the price level, caused by credit contraction.

There can, of course, be little doubt that, at the present time, a deflationary process is going on and that an indefinite continuation of that deflation would do inestimable harm. But this does not, by any means, necessarily mean that the deflation is the original cause of our difficulties or that we could overcome these difficulties by compensating for the deflationary tendencies, at present operative in our economic system, by forcing more money into circulation. There is no reason to assume that the crisis was started by a deliberate deflationary action on the part of the monetary authorities, or that the deflation itself is anything but a secondary phenomenon, a process induced by the maladjustments of industry left over from the boom. If, however, the deflation is not a cause but an effect of the unprofitableness of industry, then it is surely vain to hope that, by reversing the deflationary process, we can regain lasting prosperity. Far from following a deflationary policy, Central Banks, particularly in the United States, have been making earlier and more far-reaching efforts than have ever been undertaken before to combat the depression by a policy of credit expansion — with the result that the depression has lasted longer and has become more severe than any preceding one. What we need is a readjustment of those elements in the structure of production and of prices which existed before the deflation began and which then made it unprofitable for industry to borrow. But, instead of furthering the inevitable liquidation of the maladjustments brought about by the boom during the last three years, all conceivable means have been used to prevent that readjustment from taking place; and one of these means, which has been repeatedly tried though without success, from the earliest to the most recent stages of depression, has been this deliberate policy of credit expansion.

It is very probable that the much discussed rigidities, which had already grown up in many parts of the modern economic system before 1929, would, in any case, have made the process of readjustment much slower and more painful. It is also probable that these very resistances to

readjustment would have set up a severe deflationary process which would finally have overcome
those rigidities. To what extent, under the given
situation of a relatively rigid price and wage
system, this deflationary process is perhaps not
only inevitable but is even the quickest way of
bringing about the required result, is a very
difficult question, about which, on the basis of
our present knowledge, I should be afraid to make
any definite pronouncement.

It seems certain, however, that we shall merely
make matters worse if we aim at curing the
deflationary symptoms and, at the same time (by
the erection of trade barriers and other forms of
state intervention) do our best to increase rather
than to decrease the fundamental maladjustments.
More than that: while the advantages of such a
course are, to say the least, uncertain, the new
dangers which it creates are great. To combat the
depression by a forced credit expansion is to
attempt to cure the evil by the very means which
brought it about; because we are suffering from
a misdirection of production, we want to create
further misdirection — a procedure which can only

lead to a much more severe crisis as soon as the credit expansion comes to an end. It would not be the first experiment of this kind which has been made. We should merely be repeating, on a much larger scale, the course followed by the Federal Reserve system in 1927, an experiment which Mr. A. C. Miller, the only economist on the Federal Reserve Board and, at the same time, its oldest member, has rightly characterized as 'the greatest and boldest operation ever undertaken by the Federal reserve system', an operation which 'resulted in one of the most costly errors committed by it or any other banking system in the last 75 years'. It is probably to this experiment, together with the attempts to prevent liquidation once the crisis had come, that we owe the exceptional severity and duration of the depression. We must not forget that, for the last six or eight years, monetary policy all over the world has followed the advice of the stabilizers. It is high time that their influence, which has already done harm enough, should be overthrown.

We cannot hope for the overthrow of this alluringly simple theory until its theoretical basis is definitely refuted and something better substituted for it. The opponents of the stabilization programme still labour — and probably always will labour — under the disadvantage that they have no equally simple and clear-cut rule to propose; perhaps no rule at all which will satisfy the eagerness of those who hope to cure all evils by authoritative action. But whatever may be our hope for the future, the one thing of which we must be painfully aware at the present time — a fact which no writer on these problems should fail to impress upon his readers — is how little we really know of the forces which we are trying to influence by deliberate management; so little indeed that it must remain an open question whether we would try if we knew more.

FRIEDRICH A. HAYEK

The London School of Economics
June 1932

CHAPTER I

THE PROBLEM OF THE TRADE CYCLE

I

ANY attempt either to forecast the trend of economic development, or to influence it by measures based on an examination of existing conditions, must presuppose certain quite definite conceptions as to the necessary course of economic phenomena. Empirical studies, whether they are undertaken with such practical aims in view, or whether they are confined merely to the amplification, with the aid of special statistical devices, of our knowledge of the course of particular phases of trade fluctuations, can, at best, afford merely a verification of existing theories; they cannot, in themselves, provide new insight into the causes or the necessity of the Trade Cycle.

This view has been stated very forcibly by Professor A. Löwe.*

* In his essay: *Wie ist Konjunkturtheorie überhaupt möglich?* Weltwirtschaftliches Archiv, vol. 24. 1926 part 2, p. 166.

'Our insight into the *theoretical* interconnections of economic cycles, and into the structural laws of circulation', he says, 'has not been enriched at all by descriptive work or calculations of correlations.' We can entirely agree with him, moreover, when he goes on to say that 'to expect an immediate furtherance of *theory* from an increase in *empirical* insight is to misunderstand the logical relationship between theory and empirical research'.

The reason for this is clear. The means of perception employed in statistics are not the same as those employed in economic theory; and it is therefore impossible to fit regularities established by the former into the structure of economic laws prescribed by the latter. We cannot superimpose upon the system of fundamental propositions comprised in the theory of equilibrium, a Trade Cycle theory resting on unrelated logical foundations. All the phenomena observed in cyclical fluctuations, particularly price formation and its influence on the direction and the volume of production, have already been explained by the theory of equilibrium; they can only be integrated as an explanation of the totality of economic events by means of fundamentally similar constructions. Trade Cycle theory itself is only expected to explain how certain prices are determined, and to state their influence on production and consumption; and the determining conditions of these phenomena are already given by elementary theory. Its special task arises from the fact that these phenomena show empirically observed movements for the explanation of which the methods of equilibrium theory are as yet inadequate. One need not go so far as to say that a successful solution could be reached only in conjunction with a positive explanation of elementary phenomena; but no further proof is needed that such a solution can only be achieved in association with, or by means of, a theory which explains how certain prices or certain uses of given goods are determined at all. It is not only that we lack theories which fulfil this condition and which fall outside the category best described as 'equilibrium theories' * —

Cf. Löwe: *Der gegenwärtige Stand der Konjunkturtheorie in Deutschland*, Die Wirtschaftswissenschaft nach dem Kriege, Festgabe für Lujo Brentano zum 80. Geburtstag, vol. ii, p. 360.

theories which are characterized by taking the logic of economic action as their starting point; the point is rather that statistical method is fundamentally unsuited to this purpose. Just as no statistical investigation can prove that a given change in demand must necessarily be followed by a certain change in price, so no statistical method can explain why all economic phenomena present that regular wave-like appearance which we observe in cyclical fluctuations. This can be explained only by widening the assumptions on which our deductions are is based, so that cyclical fluctuations would follow from these as a necessary consequence, just as the general propositions of the theory of price followed from the narrower assumptions of equilibrium theory.

But even these new assumptions cannot be established by statistical investigation. The statistical approach, unlike deductive inference, leaves the conditions under which established economic relations hold good fundamentally undetermined; and similarly, the objects to which they relate cannot be determined as unequivocally as by theory. Empirically established relations between various economic phenomena continue to present a problem to theory until the necessity for their interconnections can be demonstrated independently of any statistical evidence.* The concepts on which such an explanation is based will be quite different from those by which statistical interconnections are demonstrated; they can be reached independently. Moreover, the corroboration of statistical evidence provides, in itself, no proof of correctness. *A priori* we cannot expect from statistics anything more than the stimulus provided by the indication of new problems.

In thus emphasizing the fact that Trade Cycle theory, while it may serve as a basis for statistical

---

* Cf. the excellent analysis given by E. Altschul in his well-known essay *Konjunkturtheorie und Konjunkturstatistik* (Archiv für Sozialwissenschaft und Sozialpolitik, vol. 55, Tubingen, 1926). Altschul as a statistician deserves especial credit when, recognizing the limitations of statistical methods, he writes (p. 85) 'In economics especially, the final decision about the significance of a certain phenomenon can never be left to mathematical and statistical analysis. The main approach to research must necessarily lie through theoretically obtained knowledge.' Cf. also A. C. Pigou, *Industrial Fluctuations*, 2nd ed. (London, 1929) p. 37, 'The absence of statistical correlation between a given series of changes and industrial fluctuations does not by itself disprove – and its presence does not prove – that these changes are causes of the fluctuations.'

research, can never itself be established by the latter, it is by no means desired to deprecate the value of the empirical method. On the contrary, there can be no doubt that Trade Cycle theory can only gain full practical importance through exact measurement of the actual course of the phenomena which it describes. But before we can examine the question of the true importance of statistics to theory, it must be clearly recognized that the use of statistics can never consist in a deepening of our theoretical insight.

I I

Even as a means of verification, the statistical examination of the cycles has only a very limited value for Trade Cycle theory. For the latter — as for any other economic theory — there are only two criteria of correctness. Firstly, it must be deduced with unexceptionable logic from the fundamental notions of the theoretical system; and secondly, it must explain by a purely deductive method those phenomena with all their peculiarities which we observe in the actual cycles.* Such a theory could only be 'false' either through an inadequacy in its logic or because the phenomena which it explains do not correspond with the observed facts. If, however, the theory is logically sound, and if it leads to an explanation of the given phenomena as a necessary consequence of these general conditions of economic activity, then the best that statistical investigation can do is to show that there still remains an unexplained residue of processes. It could never prove that the determining relationships are of a different character from those maintained by the theory.†

It might be shown, for instance, by statistical investigation that a general rise in prices is followed

---

* Professor A. Löwe, in his report *Uber den Einfluss monetärer Faktoren auf den Konjunkturzyklus* Schriften des Vereins für Sozialpolitik, vol. 173, part 2, p. 357) expresses his views in almost the same words. The above sentences first appeared in another article in the same volume.

† Cf. the analysis concerning 'Argument der Wirklichkeitswidrigkeit' in the recent book of E. Carell, *Sozialökonomische Theorie und Konjunkturproblem'*, München and Leipzig, 1929, for a very acute methodological argument. He opposes the thesis of Löwe (which remains, however, despite his analysis, the basis of my own work) that the incorporation of cyclical phenomena into the system of economic equilibrium theory, with which they are in apparent contradiction, remains the crucial problem of Trade Cycle theory.

by an expansion of production, and a general fall in prices by a diminution of production; but this would not necessarily mean that theory should regard the movement of price as an independent cause of movements of production. So long as a theory could explain the regular occurrence of this parallelism in any other way, it could not be disproved by statistics, even if it maintained that the connection between the two phenomena was of a precisely opposite nature.* It is therefore only in a negative sense that it is possible to verify theory by statistics. Either statistics can demonstrate that there are phenomena which the theory does not sufficiently explain, or it is unable to discover such phenomena. It cannot be expected to confirm the theory in a positive sense. The possibility is completely ruled out by what has been said above, since it would presuppose an assertion of *necessary* interconnec-

---

* A well-known instance of such an apparent contradiction between a correct theoretical assertion and experience is the connection between the level of interest rates and the movement of prices. Cf. Wicksell, *Vorlesungen*, vol. ii, 'Geld und Kredit,' Jena 1922. See also my essay, '*Das intertemporale Gleichgewichts-system der Preise und die Bewegungen des Geldweries*, (Weltwirtschaftiches Archiv, vol. 28, Jena 1928, p. 63 *et seq.*).

tions, such as statistics cannot make. There is no reason to be surprised, therefore, that although nearly all modern Trade Cycle theories use statistical material as corroboration, it is only where a given theory fails to explain all the observed phenomena that this statistical evidence can be used to judge its merits.

I I I

Thus it is not by enriching or by checking theoretical analysis that economic statistics gain their real importance. This lies elsewhere. The proper task of statistics is to give us accurate information about the events which fall within the province of theory, and so to enable us not only to connect two consecutive events as cause and effect, *a posteriori*, but to grasp existing conditions completely enough for forecasts of the future and, eventually, appropriate action, to become possible. It is only through this possibility of forecasts of systematic action that theory gains practical importance.* A theory might, for instance, enable us to infer from the comparative movements of certain prices and quantities an imminent change in the direction of those movements: but we should have little use for such a theory if we were unable to ascertain the *actual* movements of the phenomena in question. With regard to certain phenomena

* It should be noted that the idea of forecasting is by no means a new one, although it is often regarded as such. Every economic theory, and indeed all theory of whatever sort, aims exclusively at foretelling the necessary consequences of a given situation, event or measure. The subject-matter of trade cycle theory being what it is, it follows that ideally it should result in a collective forecast showing the total development resulting from a given situation under given conditions. In practice, such forecasts are attempted in too unconditional a form, and on an inadmissibly over-simplified basis; and, consequently, the very possibility of scientific judgments about future economic trends to-day appears problematical, and cautious thinkers are apt to disparage any attempt at such forecasting. In contrast to this view, we have to emphasize very strongly that statistical research in this field is meaningless except in so far as it leads to a forecast, however much that forecast may have to be hedged about with qualifications. In particular any measures aimed at alleviating the Trade Cycle (and necessarily based on statistical research) must be conceived in the light of certain assumptions as to the future trend to be expected in the absence of such measures. Statistical research, therefore, serves only to furnish the bases for the utilization of existing theoretical principles. Dr. O. Morgenstern's recent categorical denial (*Wirtschaftsprognose, Untersuchung ihrer Voraussetzungen und Möglichkeiten*, Wien, 1928) of the possibility of forecasting seems to be due only to the fact that he demands more from forecasting than is justifiable. Even the ability to forecast a hailstorm would not be useless – but, on the contrary, very valuable – if the latter could thereupon be averted by firing rockets at the clouds!

having an important bearing on the Trade Cycle, our position is a peculiar one. We can deduce from general insight how the majority of people will behave under certain conditions; but the actual behaviour of these masses at a given moment, and therefore the conditions to which our theoretical conclusions must be applied, can only be ascertained by the use of complicated statistical methods. This is especially true when a phenomenon is influenced by a number of partly known circumstances, such as, e.g., seasonal changes. Here very complicated statistical investigations are needed to ascertain whether these circumstances whose presence indicates the applicability of theoretical conclusions were in fact operative. Often statistical analysis may detect phenomena which have, as yet, no theoretical explanation, and which therefore necessitate either an extension of theoretical speculation or a search for new determining conditions. But the explanation of the phenomena thus detected, if it is to serve as a basis for forecasts of the future, must in every case utilize other methods than statistically observed regularities; and the observed phenomena will have to be deduced from the theoretical system, independently of empirical detection.

The dependence of statistical research on pre-existing theoretical explanation hardly needs further emphasis. This holds good not only as regards the practical utilization of its results, but also in the course of its working, in which it must look to theory for guidance in selecting and delimiting the phenomena to be investigated. The oft-repeated assertion that statistical examination of the Trade Cycle should be undertaken without any theoretical prejudice is therefore always based on self-deception.*

* Prof. Bullock, the Principal of the Harvard Economic Service (now the Harvard Economic Society) constantly emphasizes the complete absence of theoretical prepossession with which the work of the Institute is carried out. Sincere as this belief unquestionably is, however, one may doubt its validity when one reads, for instance, the following account given by Prof. Bullock's chief collaborator, Mr. W. M. Persons, the inventor of the famous Harvard Barometer. Here he attempts the following popular explanation of the latter:—'This account of the business cycle, based upon our statistical analysis, revolves about the fluctuation of short-time interest rates, speculation, and business. We may think of interest rates as varying inversely with the amount of the bank reserves in the credit reservoir. The flow in the supply pipe to this reservoir depends upon the volume of gold imports, gold production, and the volume of paper currency. There are two outlets from this reservoir of credit: one pipe furnishes credit for speculation in securities; the other pipe is for the flow of credit

On the whole, one can say without exaggeration that the practical value of statistical research depends primarily upon the soundness of the theoretical conceptions on which it is based. To decide upon the most important problems of the Trade Cycle remains the task of theory; and whether the money and labour so freely expended on statistical research in late years will be repaid by the expected success depends primarily on whether the development of theoretical understanding keeps pace with the exploration of the facts. For we must not deceive ourselves: not only do we now lack a theory which is generally accepted by

into business. When the level of credit in the reservoir is high, and perhaps the outlet to business is partially clogged, the flow of funds into speculation begins. After this flow goes on for some time, however, and the flow into business increases, the level of credit in the reservoir falls. Obstruction is offered to the flow into speculative markets by the devices of higher interest rates and direct discrimination against speculation and in favour of business. The outlet into speculation therefore becomes clogged but the flow into business goes on. The level in the reservoir becomes still lower until the time is reached when bankers consider it dangerous to allow the outflow to continue. We then have a halt in further credit expansion, or to use our illustration, both outlets are clogged for a time and bank reserves are brought back to normal by allowing the supply to again fill the tank.' ('A non-technical explanation of the index of general business conditions,' *The Review of Economic Statistics*, prel. vol. ii, Cambridge, 1920. p. 47).

economists, but we do not even possess one which could be formulated in such an unexceptionable way, and worked out in such detail, as eventually to command such acceptance. A series of important interconnections have been established and some principles of the greatest significance expounded; but no one has yet undertaken the decisive step which creates a complete theory by using one of these principles to incorporate all the known phenomena into the existing system in a satisfactory way. To realize this, of course, does not hinder us from pursuing either economic research or economic policy; but then we must always remember that we are acting on certain theoretical assumptions whose correctness has not yet been satisfactorily established. The 'practical man' habitually acts on theories which he does not consciously realize; and in most cases this means that his theories are fallacious. Using a theory consciously, on the other hand, always results in some new attempt to clear up the interrelations which it assumes, and to bring it into harmony with which theoretical assumptions; that is, it results in the pursuit of theory for its own sake.

I V

The value of business forecasting depends upon correct theoretical concepts; hence there can, at the present time, be no more important task in this field than the bridging of the gulf which divides monetary from non-monetary theories.* This gulf leads to differences of opinion in the front rank of economists; and is also the characteristic line of division between Trade Cycle theory in Germany and in America — where business forecasting originated. Such an analysis of the relation between these two main trends seems to me especially important because

---

* Since the publication of the German edition of this book, I have become less convinced that the difference between monetary and non-monetary explanations is *the most important* point of disagreement between the various Trade Cycle theories. On the one hand, it seems to me that within the monetary group of explanations the difference between those theorists who regard the superficial phenomena of changes in the value of money as decisive factors in determining cyclical fluctuations, and those who lay emphasis on the real changes in the structure of production brought about by monetary causes, is much greater than the difference between the latter group and such so-called non-monetary theorists as Prof. Spiethoff and Prof. Cassel. On the other hand, it seems to me that the difference between these explanations, which seek the cause of the crisis in the scarcity of capital, and the so-called 'under-consumption' theories, is theoretically as well as practically of much more far-reaching importance than the difference between monetary and non-monetary theories.

of the peculiar position of the monetary theories. Largely through the fault of some of their best-known advocates in Germany, monetary explanations became discredited, and their essentials have, moreover, been much misunderstood; while, on the other hand, the reaction against them forms the main reason for the prevailing scepticism as to the possibility of any economic theory of the Trade Cycle — a scepticism which may seriously retard the development of theoretical research.*

There is a fundamental difficulty inherent in all Trade Cycle theories which take as their starting point an empirically ascertained disturbance of the equilibrium of the various branches of production. This difficulty arises because, in stating the effects of that disturbance, they have to make use of the logic of equilibrium theory.† Yet this logic, properly followed through, can do no more

* Cf. the above-mentioned essay of A. Löwe in the 'Weltwirtschaftliches Archiv.'

† By 'equilibrium theory' we here primarily understand the modern theory of the general interdependence of all economic quantities, which has been most perfectly expressed by the Lausanne School of theoretical economics. The significant basic concept of this theory was contained in James Mill's and J. B. Say's *Théorie des Débouchés*. Cf. L. Miksch, *Gibt es eine allgemeine Überproduktion?* Jena, 1929.

than demonstrate that such disturbances of equilibrium can come only from outside — i.e. that they represent a change in the economic data — and that the economic system always reacts to such changes by its well-known methods of adaptation, i.e. by the formation of a new equilibrium. No tendency towards the special expansion of certain branches of production, however plausibly adduced, no chance shift in demand, in distribution or in productivity, could adequately explain, within the framework of this theoretical system, why a general 'disproportionality' between supply and demand should arise. For the essential means of explanation in static theory, which is, at the same time, the indispensable assumption for the explanation of particular price variations, is the assumption that prices supply an automatic mechanism for equilibrating supply and demand.

The next section will deal with these difficulties in more detail: a mere hint should therefore be sufficient at this point. At the moment we have only to draw attention to the fact that the problem before us cannot be solved by examining the effect of a certain cause within the framework, and by the methods, of equilibrium theory. Any theory which limits itself to the explanation of empirically observed interconnections by the methods of elementary theory necessarily contains a self-contradiction. For Trade Cycle theory cannot aim at the adaptation of the adjusting mechanism of static theory to a special case; this scheme of explanation must itself be extended so as to explain how such discrepancies between supply and demand can ever arise. The obvious, and (to my mind) the only possible way out of this dilemma, is to explain the difference between the course of events described by static theory (which only permits movements towards an equilibrium, and which is deduced by directly contrasting the supply of and the demand for goods) and the actual course of events, by the fact that, with the introduction of money (or strictly speaking with the introduction of indirect exchange), a new determining cause is introduced. Money being a commodity which, unlike all others, is incapable of finally satisfying demand, its introduction does away with the rigid interdependence and self-sufficiency of the 'closed' system of equilibrium, and makes possible movements which would be excluded from the latter. Here we have a starting-point which fulfils the essential conditions for any satisfactory theory of the Trade Cycle. It shows, in a purely deductive way, the possibility and the necessity of movements which *do not* at any given moment tend towards a situation which, in the absence of changes in the economic 'data', could continue indefinitely. It shows that, on the contrary, these movements lead to such a 'disproportionality' between certain parts of the system that the given situation cannot continue.

But while it seems that it was a sound instinct which led economists to begin by looking on the monetary side for an explanation of cyclical fluctuations, it also seems probable that the one-sided development of the theory of money has, as yet, prevented any satisfactory solution to the problem being found. Monetary theories of the Trade Cycle succeeded in giving prominence to the right questions and, in many cases, made important contributions towards their solution; but the reason why an unassailable solution has not yet been put forward seems to reside in the fact that all the adherents of the monetary theory of the Trade Cycle have sought an explanation either exclusively or predominantly in the superficial phenomena of changes in the value of money, while failing to pursue the far more profound and fundamental effects of the process by which money is introduced into the economic system, as distinct from its effect on prices in general. Nor did they follow up the consequences of the fundamental diversity between a money economy and the pure barter economy which is assumed in static theory.*

V

Naturally it cannot be the business of this essay to remove all defects and deficiencies from the monetary theories of the Trade Cycle, or to develop a complete and unassailable theory. In these pages I shall only attempt to show the general significance for this theory of the monetary starting-point, and to refute the most important

* Similar views are expressed by W. Röpke, *Kredit und Konjunktur. Jahrbücher für Nationalökonomie und Statistik*, 3rd series, vol. 69, pp. 264 *et seq.*

objections raised against the monetary explanation by proving that certain rightly exposed deficiencies of some monetary theories do not necessarily follow from the monetary approach. All that is wanted, therefore, is, first, a proof, using as our examples some of the best-known non-monetary theories, that the 'real' explanations adduced by them do not, in themselves, suffice to build up a complete and consistent theory; secondly, a demonstration that the existing monetary theories contain the germ of a true explanation, although all suffer, more or less, from that over-simplification of the problem which results from reducing all cyclical fluctuations to fluctuations in the value of money; finally that the monetary starting-point makes it possible, in fact, to show deductively the inevitability of fluctuation under the existing monetary system and, indeed, under almost any other which can be imagined. It will be shown, in particular, that the Wicksell-Mises theory of the effects of a divergence between the 'natural' and the money rate of interest already contains the most important elements of an explanation, and has only to be freed from any direct reference to a purely imaginary 'general money value' (as has already been partly done by Prof. Mises) in order to form the basis of a Trade Cycle theory sufficing for a deductive explanation of all the elements in the Trade Cycle.

CHAPTER II

NON-MONETARY THEORIES
OF THE TRADE CYCLE

I

ANY attempt at a general proof, within the compass
of a short essay, of the assertion that non-monetary
theories of the Trade Cycle inevitably suffer from
a fundamental deficiency, appears to be confronted
with an insuperable obstacle by reason of the very
multiplicity of such theories. If it were necessary
for our purpose to show that every one of the
numerous disequilibrating forces which have been
made starting-points for Trade Cycle theories
was, in fact, non-existent, then the conditions of
our success would, indeed, be impossible of
fulfilment; for not only would it be almost impossible to deal with all extant theories but no conclu-
sive answer could result, seeing that we should still
have to reckon with a new and hitherto unrefuted
crop of such theories in the future. Moreover,

the existence of most of the interconnections elaborated by the various Trade Cycle theories can hardly be denied, and our task is rather their co-ordination in a unified logical structure than the development of entirely new and different trains of thought. In fact, it is by no means necessary to question the material correctness of the individual interconnections emphasized in the various non-monetary theories in order to show that they do not afford a sufficient explanation. As has already been indicated in the first chapter, none of them is able to overcome the contradiction between the course of economic events as described by them and the fundamental ideas of the theoretical system which they have to utilize in order to explain that course. It will, therefore, be sufficient to show, by examination of some of the best-known theories, that they do not answer this fundamental question; nor can they ever do so by their present methods and by reference to the circumstances which they now regard as relevant to Trade-Cycle theory. When, however, the question is answered on different lines, viz., by reference to *monetary* circumstances, it can be shown that the elements of explanation adduced by different theories lose their independent importance and fall into a subordinate position as necessary consequences of the monetary cause.

It is rather difficult to select the main types of Trade-Cycle theory for this purpose, since we have no theoretically satisfactory classification. The latest attempts at such classifications, by Mr. W. M. Persons,* Professor W. C. Mitchell,† and Mr. A. H. Hansen,‡ show that the usual division, which relies on external features and hardly touches the solution of fundamental problems, gives far too wide a scope for arbitrary decisions. As Professor Löwe§ has correctly emphasized (and as should be obvious from what has been said above) the only classification which could be really unobjectionable would be one which proceded according to the manner in which such theories explain the absence of the 'normal course' of economic events, as pre-

---

*'Theories of Business Fluctuations' (*Quarterly Journal of Economics*, vol. xli, p. 923).

† *Business Cycles: the Problem and its Setting* (New York 1927).

‡ *Business Cycle Theory: its Development and present Status* (Boston, 1927).

§ See *Der Gegenwärtige Stand der Konjunkturforschung*, p. 359 *et seq.*

sented by static theory. In fact, the various theories—as we shall hope to show later — make no attempt whatever to do this. As there is, therefore, no classification which would serve our purpose, our choice must be more or less arbitrary; but by choosing some of the best known theories and exemplifying the train of thought to which our objection particularly applies, we should be able to make the general validity of the latter sufficiently clear. The task is made rather easier by the fact that there does exist to-day, on at least one point, a far-reaching agreement among the different theories. They all regard the emergence of a *disproportionality* among the various productive groups, and in particular the excessive production of capital goods, as the first and main thing to be explained. The development of theory owes a real debt to statistical research in that, to-day, there is at least no substantial disagreement as to the thing to be explained.

There is, however, a point to be emphasized here. The modern habit of going beyond the actual crisis and seeking to explain the entire cycle, suffers inherently from the danger of paying less and less attention to the crucial problem. In particular, the attempt to give the object of the theory as neutral a name as possible (such as 'Industrial fluctuations' or 'Cyclical movements of Industry') threatens to drive the real theoretical problem more into the background than was the case in the old theory of crisis. The simple fact that economic development does not go on quite uniformly, but that periods of relatively rapid change alternate with periods of relative stagnation, does not in itself constitute a problem. It is sufficiently explained by the adjustment of the economic system to irregular changes in the data — changes whose occurrence we always have to assume and which cannot be further explained by economic science. The real problem presented to economic theory is: Why does not this adjustment come about smoothly and continuously, just as a new equilibrium is formed after every change in the data? Why is there this temporary possibility of developments leading away from equilibrium and finally, without any changes in data, necessitating a change in the economic trend? The phenomena of the upward trend of the cycle and of the culminating boom constitute a problem only because they inevitably bring about a slump in sales — i.e. a falling-off of economic activity — which is *not* occasioned by any corresponding change in the original economic data.

II

The prevailing disproportionality theories are in agreement in one respect. They all see the cause of the slump in the fact that, during the boom, for various reasons, the productive apparatus is expanded more than is warranted by the corresponding flow of consumption; there finally appears a scarcity of finished consumption goods, thus causing a rise in the price of such goods relatively to the price of production goods (which amounts to the same thing as a rise in the rate of interest) so that it becomes unprofitable to employ the enlarged productive apparatus or, in many cases, even to complete it. At present there is hardly a recognized theory which does not give this idea, which we only sketch for the moment,*

* Cf. below, p. 212 *et seq.* esp. p. 217.

a decisive place in its argument, and we should therefore be well advised to begin by seeing how the various theories try to deal with the phenomenon in question. Apart from the monetary theories, which, as will be shown later, *can only be considered satisfactory if they explain that phenomenon*, there are two groups of explanations which can be entirely disregarded. In the first place there is nothing to be gained from an examination of those theories which seek to explain cyclical fluctuations by corresponding cyclical changes in certain external circumstances, while merely using the unquestionable methods of equilibrium theory to explain the economic phenomena which follow from these changes. To decide on the correctness of these theories is beyond the competence of Economics. In the second place, it is best, for the moment, to exclude from consideration those theories whose argument depends so entirely on the assumption of monetary changes that when the latter are excluded no systematic explanation is left. This category includes Professor J. Schumpeter,* Pro-

* *Theorie der wirtschaftlichen Entwicklung*, 2nd edit., Müchen and Leipzig, 1926.

57

fessor E. Lederer,* and Professor G. Cassel,† and to a certain extent Professor W. C. Mitchell and Professor J. Lescure.‡ We shall have to consider later, with regard to this category, how far it is theoretically permissible to treat these monetary interconnections as determining conditions on the same footing as the other phenomena used in explanation.

It is, of course, impossible at this point to go into the peculiarities of all types of theory, as worked out by their respective authors. We must leave out of account the forms in which the various explanations are presented, and confine ourselves to certain underlying types of theory which recur in a number of different guises. Inevitably, this treatment of contemporary theories must fail to do full justice to the intellectual merits exemplified in each; but for the purposes

---

* *Konjunktur und Krisen: Grundriss der Sozialökonomik*, Abt. IV, Teil I. Tübingen 1926; also *Zur Morphologie der Krisen* in *Die Wirtschaftstheorie der Gegenwart*, cited above, edited by H. Mayer, vol iv, Vienna, 1928.

† Theory of Social Economy.

‡ *Des Crises générales et périodiques de surproduction*. Paris, 1913; and *Krisenlehre* in *Die Wirtschaftstheorie der Gegenwart*, ed. by H. Mayer, vol. iv, Vienna 1928.

of this chapter — that is, to show the fundamental objections to which all non-monetary theories of the Trade Cycle are open — this somewhat cursory and imperfect treatment may be enough.

We may begin our demonstration by pointing out that all those forms of disproportionality theory with which we have to deal here rest on the existence of quite irregular fluctuations of 'economic data' (that is, the external determining circumstances of the economic system, including human needs and abilities). From this assumption, they try to explain in one way or another that the fluctuations in consumption or some other element in the economic system occasioned by these changes are followed by relatively greater changes in the production of production goods.* These wide fluctuations in the industries making production goods bring about a disproportionality between them and the consumption industries

---

* It should be noted here that the assumption of initial changes in the economic data, which no theory of the Trade Cycle can dispense with, in itself throws no light on the proper way of explaining cyclical fluctuations. It is not the occurrence of disturbances of equilibrium, necessitating readjustment, which presents a problem to Trade Cycle theory; it is the fact that this adjustment is brought about only after a series of movements have taken place which cannot be considered

to such an extent that a reversal of the movement becomes necessary. *It is not, therefore, the simple fact of fluctuation in the production of capital goods (which is certainly inevitable in the course of economic growth) which has to be explained.* The real problem is the growth of excessive fluctuations in the capital goods industries out of the inevitable and irregular fluctuations of the rest of the economic system, and the disproportional development, arising from these, of the two main branches of production. We can distinguish three main types of non-monetary theories explaining the exaggerated effect of given fluctuations on capital goods industries. The most common, at the moment, are those explanations which try to show that, on account of the *technique of production*, an increase in the demand for consumption goods, whether expected

'adjustments' in the sense used by the theory of economic equilibrium. 'The phenomenon is never made clear until it is explained why its cause, whatever it may be, does not call forth a continuous equilibrating process' (Prof. J. Schumpeter, Theorie der wirtschaftlichen Entwicklung, 2nd ed., München and Leipzig, 1926). These changes of data could serve as a complete explanation only if it could be shown that the successive phases of the Trade Cycle are conditioned by a series of such changes, following each other in a certain order.

or actual, tends to bring about a relatively larger increase in the production of goods of a higher order, either generally or in a certain group of these goods. Hardly less common, and differing only in appearance, are explanations which seek to derive these augmented fluctuations from special circumstances (non-monetary in character) arising in the field of *savings and investment.* Finally, as a third group, we must mention certain *psychological* theories, which, for the most part, have however no pretension to rank as independent explanations and which merely reinforce other arguments, and are open to the same objections as the two other main types.

I I I

We shall mention only the most important of our objections to the first type, which is the easiest to discuss from this point of view. It is common to so many economists that it is hardly necessary to mention particular representatives. The simplest way of deductively explaining excessive fluctuations in the production of capital goods is by reference to the *long period of time* which is necessary, under modern conditions, for preparing the fixed capital goods which enable the expansion of the productive process to take place.* According to a widely held view, this circumstance alone is enough to make every increase in the sales of consumption goods, whether brought about by an intensification of demand or by a fall in the costs of production, capable of bringing about a more than proportional increase in the production of intermediary goods. This is explained either by the individual producer's ignorance of what his competitors are doing, or — as is common in American writings — by the 'cumulative effect' of each change in the sale of consumption goods on the higher stages of production. Owing to circumstances which will be explained later, the leading idea in all these types of explanation is that the long period which, with the present technique of production, elapses between the beginning of a productive process and

* Cf. A. Aftalion: *Les crises périodiques de surproduction*, Paris, 1913, Bks. ii-vi, Chaps. III to VIII; and D. H. Robertson, *Industrial Fluctuations*. London, 1915, p. 14.

the arrival of its final product at the market, prevents the gradual adjustment of production to changes in demand through the agency of prices and makes it possible, from time to time, for an excessively large supply to be thrown on the market. This idea is supported by another, which however, can be independently and more widely applied; that is, that *every change in demand*, from the moment of its appearance, *propagates itself cumulatively* through all the grades of production, from the lowest to the highest. This cumulative effect arises because at each stage, besides the change which would be appropriate to the actual shift in demand, another change arises from the adjustment of stocks and of productive apparatus to the alteration in market conditions.* An increase in the demand for consumption goods will not merely call forth a proportional increase in the demand for goods of a higher order: the latter will also be increased by the amount needed to raise current stocks to a

† Cf. T. N. Carver, *Quarterly Journal of Economics*, 1903-4, p. 492; A. Aftalion, *Journal d'Economie Politique*, 1909, pp. 215 *ff.*; W. C. Mitchell, *op. cit.*; and D. H. Robertson, *op. cit.*, p. 122 *ff.*

proportional level, and, finally, by the further amount by which the requirements for producing new means of production exceed those for keeping the existing means of production intact. (For instance, an extension of 10 per cent, in one particular year, in the machinery of a factory which normally renews 10 per cent of its machinery annually, causes an increase of 100 per cent in the production of machinery — i.e. a given increase in the demand for consumption goods occasions a tenfold increase in the production of production-goods.) This idea is offered as an adequate reason not only for the relatively greater fluctuations in production-goods industries but also for their *excessive* expansion in periods of boom. Similarly, the extensive use of *durable capital equipment* in the modern economy is often singled out for responsibility.* Industries using heavy equipment are prone to excessive expansion in boom periods because small increments in this equipment are impossible; expansion must necessarily take place by sudden jerks. Once the new equipment is available, on the other hand, the

* Cf. D. H. Robertson: *op. cit.*, pp. 31 *et seq.*

64

volume of production has little influence on total costs, which go on even if no production takes place at all. New inventions and new needs, however, although they are often adduced as explaining the accelerated and excessive growth of capital goods industries, cannot be dealt with on the same footing. They only represent a special group of the many possible causes from which the cumulative processes described above may originate.

I V

There is virtually no doubt that all these interconnections, and many others which are given prominence in various Trade Cycle theories and which similarly tend to disturb economic equilibrium, do actually exist; and any Trade Cycle theory which claims to be comprehensively worked out must take them into consideration. But none of them get over the real difficulty — namely: Why do the forces tending to restore equilibrium become temporarily ineffective and why do they only come into action again when it is too late? They all try to explain this phenomenon by a further, usually tacit, assumption, which one of the advocates of these theories, Mr. C. O. Hardy,* has himself put forward as their common idea, by which, in my opinion, he brings out, with the utmost clarity, their fundamental weakness. He states that all those theories which are based on the length of the production-period under modern technical conditions agree in regarding these conditions as a source of difficulty to producers in adjusting production to the state of the market; producing, as they must, for a future period, the market possibilities of which are necessarily unknown to them. He then emphasises that in general it is the task of the price-mechanism to adjust supply to demand; he thinks, however, that this mechanism is imperfect, if a long period has to lapse between production and the arrival of the product at the market, because 'prices and orders give information concerning the prospective state of demand compared with the known facts of the present and future supply,

* *Risk and Risk Bearing*, University of Chicago Press, 1923, p. 72. See also Mr. Hardy's reply to the above criticism in the revised 2nd Edition (1931), of the same book (p. 94), which, however, does not seem to solve the fundamental difficulty.

but they give no clue to the changes in supply which they themselves are likely to cause.'* He tries to show how periodic over- and under-production may result from an increase in demand acting as an incentive to increased production. He here states explicitly what others assume tacitly, and thus his exposition completely gives away the question-begging nature of all such arguments. For he holds that under free competition, in the case considered, more and more people try to profit by the favourable situation, all ignoring one another's preparations, and '*no force intervenes to check the continual increase in production until it reflects itself in declining orders and falling prices.*'† In this statement (according to which the price-mechanism comes into action only when the products come on to the market, while, until then, producers can regulate the extent of their production solely according to the estimated *total volume of demand*) the fundamental error which can be shown to recur in all these theories is plainly revealed. It arises from a misconception of the deliberations which regulate

* *Op. cit.*, p. 73.   † Ibid. (My italics.)

the entrepreneur's actions and of the significance of the price-mechanism.

If the entrepreneur really had to guide his decisions exclusively by his knowledge of the quantitative increase in the total demand for his product, and if the success of economic activity were really always dependent on that knowledge, no very complicated circumstances would be needed to produce constant disturbances in the relation between supply and demand. But the entrepreneur in a capitalist economy is not — as many economists seem to assume — in the same situation as the dictator of a Socialist economy. The protagonists of this view seem to overlook the fact that production is generally guided not by any knowledge of the actual size of the total demand, but by the price to be obtained in the market. In the modern exchange economy, the entrepreneur does not produce with a view to satisfying a certain demand — even if that phrase is sometimes used — but on the basis of a calculation of profitability; and it is just that calculation which will equilibrate supply and demand. He is not in the least concerned with the amount by which, in a given case, the total amount demanded will alter; he only looks at the price which he can expect to get after the change in question has taken place. None of the theories under discussion explains why these expectations should generally prove incorrect. (To deduce their incorrectness from the fact that over-production, arising from false expectations, causes prices to fall, would be mere argument in a circle.) Nor can this generalization be theoretically established by any other method. For so long, at least, as disturbing monetary influences are not operating, we have to assume that the price which entrepreneurs expect to result from a change in demand or from a change in the conditions of production will more or less coincide with the equilibrium price. For the entrepreneur, from his knowledge of the conditions of production and the market, will generally be in a position to estimate the price that will rule after the changes have taken place, as distinct from the quantitative changes in the total volume of demand. One can only say, as to this prospective price of the product concerned, that it is just as likely to be lower than the equilibrium price as to be higher and that, on the average, it should more or less coincide, since there is no reason to assume that deviations will take place only in one direction. But this prospective price only represents one factor determining the extent of production. The other factor, no less important but all too often overlooked, is the price the producer has to pay for raw materials, labour-power, tools and borrowed capital — i.e. his costs. These prices, taken together, determine the extent of production for all producers operating under conditions of competition; and the producer's decisions as to his production must be guided not only by changes in expectations as to the price of his product, but also by changes in his costs. To show how the interplay of these prices keeps supply and demand, production and consumption, in equilibrium, is the main object of pure economics, and the analysis cannot be repeated here in detail. It is, however, the task of Trade Cycle theory to show under what conditions a break may occur in that tendency towards equilibrium which is described in pure analysis — i.e. why prices, in contradiction to the conclusions of static theory, do not bring about such changes in the quantities produced as would correspond to an equilibrium situation. In order to show that the theories under discussion do not solve this problem, and only as far as is necessary for this purpose, we shall now study the most important of the interconnections which bring about equilibrium under the assumptions of static theory.

V

We may attempt this task by asking what kind of reactions will be brought about by the original change in the economic data, which is supposed to cause the excessive extension of the production of capital goods, and how, in such cases, a new equilibrium can result. Whether the original impetus comes from the demand side or the supply side, the assumption from which we have to start is always a price — or rather an expected price — which renders it profitable, under the new conditions, to extend production. As stated above, we can assume — since none of the theories in question give any reason to the contrary — that this expected price will approximate to the new equilibrium price. We can assume, that is, that if the impetus is a fall in unit costs, the producer will consider the effects of an increased supply; if the impetus is an increase in demand, he will consider the increase in the cost per unit following the increase in the quantity produced. The existence of a general misconception in this respect would require a special explanation, and unless this is to rest on a circular argument, it can only be accounted for by a monetary explanation, which we cannot consider at this point.

Now the length of time required to produce modern means of production cannot induce a tendency to an excessive extension of the productive apparatus; or, more accurately, any such tendency is bound to be effectively eliminated by the increase in price of the factors of production. Thus we cannot give a sufficient explanation for the occurrence of the disproportionality in these terms. This becomes obvious as soon as we drop the assumption that the price-mechanism begins to function only from the moment at which the increased supply comes on the market, and consider that whenever the price obtainable for the finished product is correctly estimated, the adjustment of the prices of factors of production must ensure that the amount produced is limited to what can be sold at remunerative prices. The mere existence of a lengthy production period cannot be held to impair the working of the price mechanism, so long, at any rate as no additional reason can be given for the occurrence of a general miscalculation in the same direction concerning the effect of the original change in data on the prices of the products.

We must next inquire what truth there is in the alleged tendency towards a cumulative propagation of the effect of every increase (or decrease) of demand from the lower to the higher stages of production. The arguments given below against this frequently-adduced theory must serve at the same time to refute all other theories based on similar technical considerations; for space will not permit us to go into every one of these, and the reader can be trusted to apply the same reasoning as is employed in this demonstration to all similar explanations — such as those based on the necessary discontinuity of the extension of productive apparatus. Does the cumulative effect of every increase in demand represent a new price-determining factor, as a result of which prices, and therefore quantities produced, will be different from those needed to achieve equilibrium? Is the regulating effect of prices on the extent of production really suspended by the fact that when turnover increases merchants try to increase stocks, and manufacturers to extend production? If the increase in the prices of production goods were the only counterbalancing factor to set against the increase in the demand for these goods, it would still be possible for more investments to be undertaken than would prove permanently profitable. According to the view we are considering, there will be an increase in the quantity of factors of production demanded at any price, as compared with the equilibrium situation, and therefore it would appear possible that, at every price at which producers still think they can profitably make use of this quantity, investments will be undertaken to an unwarrantable extent.

This way of stating the position, however, entirely overlooks the fact that every attempt to extend the productive apparatus must necessarily bring about, besides the rise in factor prices, a further checking force — viz. a rise in the rate of interest. This greatly strengthens the effect of the rise in factor prices. It makes a greater margin between factor-prices and product-prices necessary just when this margin threatens to diminish. The maintenance of equilibrium is thus further secured.

For we must not forget that not only the volume of current production, but also the size, at any given moment, of the productive apparatus, (including stocks, which cannot be omitted) is regulated through prices, and especially — apart from the above-mentioned prices for goods and services — by the price paid for the use of capital, that is, interest. Whatever particular explanation of interest we may accept, all contemporary theories agree in regarding the function of interest as one of equalizing the supply of capital and the demand arising in various branches of production. Until some special reason can be adduced why it should not fulfil this function in any given case, we have to assume, in accordance with the fundamental thesis of static theory, that it always keeps the supply of capital goods in equilibrium with that of consumption goods. This assumption is just as indispensable, and just as inevitable, as a starting-point, as the main assumption that the supply of and demand for any kind of goods will be equilibrated by movements in the prices of those goods. In our case, when we are considering a tendency to enlarge the productive apparatus and the size of stocks, this function must be performed in such a way as to increase the rate of interest, and hence the necessary margin of profit between the price of the products and that of the means of production. This, however, automatically excludes that part of the increase in the demand for productive goods, which would have been satisfied despite the increase in their prices if the rise in the rate of interest had not taken place. None of the various Trade Cycle theories based on some alleged peculiarity of the technique of production can even begin to explain why the equilibrium position, determined by the various above-mentioned processes of price formation, should be reached at a different point from where it would be without these peculiarities.

Now as regards the prices of goods and services used for productive purposes, there seems to be no reason why they should not fulfil their function of equilibrating supply and demand. For supply and demand are here in direct relation with one another, so that any discrepancy which may arise between them, at a given price must, directly and immediately, lead to a change in that price. Only when we come to consider the second group of prices (those paid for borrowed capital or, in other words, interest) is it conceivable that disturbances might creep in, since, in this case, price formation does not act directly, by equalizing the marginal demand for and supply of capital goods, but indirectly, through its effect on money capital, whose supply need not correspond to that of real capital. But the process by which divergences can arise between these two is left unexplained by all the theories with which we have hitherto dealt. Yet before going on to see how far interest may present such a breach in the strict system of equilibrium as may serve to explain cyclical disturbances, we must briefly examine the explanation offered by the second important group of non-monetary theories, which attempt to explain the origin of periodical disturbances of equilibrium purely through the phenomena arising out of the accumulation and investment of saving.*

V I

The earlier versions of these theories start from the groundless and inadmissible assumption that unused savings are accumulated for a time and then suddenly invested, thus causing the productive apparatus to be extended in jerks. Such versions can be passed over without further analysis. For one thing, it is impossible to give any plausible explanation why unused savings should accumulate for a time;† for another thing,

* In revising the above paragraphs my notice has been called to the fact that they are in many respects in accordance with the reasoning of S. Budge in his *Grundzüge der theoretischen Nationalökonomie* (Jena, 1925, pp. 201 *et seq.*) to which I should therefore like to call attention.

† Cf. the very effective remarks of W. Eucken in his interesting viva-voce report to the Zurich Assembly of the 'Verein für Sozial-politik'. (Schriften, 175, p. 295 *et seq.*)

even if such an explanation were forthcoming, it would provide no clue to the disproportional development in the production of capital goods. The fact that the mere existence of fluctuations in saving activity does not in itself explain this problem is realized (in contrast to many other economists) by the most distinguished exponent of these theories, Prof. A. Spiethoff. This is plain from his negative answer to the analogous question, whether in a barter economy an increase in saving can create the necessary conditions for depression.* Indeed, it is difficult to see how spontaneous variations in the volume of saving (which are not themselves open to further economic explanation, and must therefore be regarded as changes of data) within the limits in which they are actually observed can possibly create the typical disturbances with which Trade Cycle theory is concerned.†

---

* 'Krisen' in *Handwörterbuch der Staatswissenschaften*, 4th ed., vol. vi, 1925, p. 81.

† It is, however, not inconceivable, theoretically, that sudden and violent fluctuations in the volume of saving might give rise to the phenomena of a crisis during their downward swings. On this point, see below Chap. v, p. 205.

Where, then, according to these theories, may we find the reason for this genesis of disequilibrating disturbances in the processes of saving and investment? We will keep to the basis of Spiethoff's theory, which is certainly the most complete of its kind. We may disregard his simple reference to the 'complexity of capital relations', for it does not in itself provide an explanation. The main basis of his explanation is to be found in the following sentence: 'If capitalists and producers of immediate consumption goods want to keep their production in step with the supply of acquisitive loan capital, these processes should be *consciously adjusted to one another*'.* But the creation of acquisitive loan capital ensues independently of the production of intermediate goods and durable capital goods; and conversely, the latter can be produced without the entrepreneur knowing the extent to which acquisitive capital (i.e. savings) exists and is available for investment;

* *Op. cit.*, p. 76. My italics. The same general view, though in a somewhat different connection, has since been expressed by Mr. J. M. Keynes in several passages of his *Treatise on Money*, 1930. Cf., for example, vol. i, p. 175 and especially p. 279: 'There is, indeed, no possibility of intelligent foresight designed to equate savings and investment unless it is exercised by the banking system.'

and thus there is always a danger that one of these processes may lag behind while the other hastens forward. This reference to the entrepreneur's ignorance of the situation belongs, however, to that category of explanation which we had to reject earlier. Instead of showing why prices — and in this case, particularly, the price of capital, which is interest — do not fulfil, or fail to fulfil adequately, their normal function of regulating the volume of production, it unexpectedly overlooks the fact that the extent of production is regulated on the basis not of a knowledge of demand but through price determination. Assuming that the rate of interest always determines the point to which the available volume of savings enables productive plant to be extended — and is it only by this assumption that we can explain what determines the rate of interest at all — any allegations of a discrepancy between savings and investments must be backed up by a demonstration why, in the given case, interest does not fulfil this function.* Professor Spiethoff,

* Elements of the same reasoning can also be found in G. Cassel *Theory of Social Economy*, 4th German edition, 1927, p. 575; when

like most of the theorists of this group, evades this necessary issue — as we shall see later — by introducing another assumption of crucial importance. It is only by means of this assumption that the causes which he particularly enumerates in his analysis gain significance as an explanation; and therefore it should not have been treated as a self-evident condition, to be casually mentioned, but as the starting-point of the whole theoretical analysis.

V I I

Before going into this question, however, we must turn our attention to the importance in Trade Cycle theory of *errors of forecast*, and, in connection with these, to a third group of theories which have not been considered up to now — the *psychological theories*. Here, as elsewhere in our investigations, we shall only be concerned with those theories which are *endogenous — i.e.*

he derives high-conjuncture from an overestimate of the supply of capital (i.e. savings) which is available to take over the supply of real capital produced.

which explain the origin of general under- and over-estimation from the economic situation itself, and not from some external circumstance such as weather changes, etc. As we said earlier, fluctuations of economic activity which merely represent an adjustment to corresponding changes in external circumstances present no problem to economic theory. The various psychological factors cited are only relevant to our analysis in so far as they can cast light on its central problem: that is, how an over-estimate of future demand can occasion a development of the productive apparatus so excessive as automatically to lead to a reaction, unprecipitated by other psychological changes. Those who are familiar with the most distinguished of these theories, that of Professor A. C. Pigou (which, owing to lack of space, cannot be reproduced here)* will see at once that the endogenous psychological theories are open to the same objections as the two groups of theories which we have already examined. Professor Pigou does

* Cf. A. C. Pigou, *Industrial Fluctuations*, London, 1927 (2nd ed. 1929); and also O. Morgenstern, *Qualitative und Quantitative Konjunkturforschung, Zeitschrift für die gesammte Staatswissenschaft*, vol. 84, Tübingen, 1928.

not explain why errors should arise in estimating the effect, on the price of the final product, of an increase in demand or a fall in cost; or, if the estimate is correct, why the readjustment of the prices of means of production should not check the expansion of production at the right point. No one would deny, of course, that errors can arise as regards the future movements of particular prices. But it is not permissible to assume without further proof that the equilibrating mechanism of the economic system will begin its work only when the excessively increased product due to these mistaken forecasts actually comes on the market, the disproportional development continuing undisturbed up to that time. At one point or another, all theories which start to explain cyclical fluctuations by miscalculations or ignorance as regards the economic situation fall into the same error as those naive explanations which base themselves on the 'planlessness' of the economic system. They overlook the fact that, in the exchange economy, production is governed by prices, independently of any knowledge of the whole process on the part of individual producers, so that it is only when the pricing process is itself disturbed that a misdirection of production can occur. The 'wrong' prices, on the other hand, which lead to 'wrong' dispositions, cannot in turn be explained by a mistake. Within the framework of a system of explanations in which, as in all modern economic theory, prices are merely expressions of a necessary tendency towards a state of equilibrium, it is not permissible to reintroduce the old Sismondian idea of the misleading effect of prices on production without first bringing it into line with the fundamental system of explanation.

VIII

It is, perhaps, scarcely necessary to point out that all the objections raised against the non-monetary theories, already cited in our investigations, are justified by one particular assumption which we had to make in order to examine the independent validity of the so-called 'real' explanations. In order to see whether the 'real' causes (whose effect is always emphasized as a proof that monetary changes are not the cause of cyclical fluctuations) can provide a sufficient explanation of the cycle, it has been necessary to study their operation under conditions of pure barter. And even if it were impossible to prove fully that, under these conditions, no non-monetary explanation is sufficient, enough has been said, I think, to indicate the general trend of thought which would refute all theories based exclusively on productive, market, financial or psychological phenomena. None of these phenomena can help us to dissolve the fundamental equilibrium-relationships which form the basis of all economic explanation. And this dissolution is indispensable if we are to protect ourselves against objections such as those outlined above.

If the various theories comprised in these groups are still able to offer a plausible explanation of cyclical fluctuations, and if their authors do not realize the contradictions involved, this is due to the unconscious importation of an assumption incompatible with a purely 'real' explanation. This assumption is adequate to dissolve the rigid reaction-mechanisms of barter-economy, and thus makes possible the processes described; but for this very reason it should not be treated as a self-evident condition, but as the basis of the explanation itself. The condition thus tacitly assumed — and one can easily prove that it is in fact assumed in all the theories examined above — is *the existence of credit* which, within reasonable limits, is always at the entrepreneur's disposal at an unchanged price. This, however, assumes the absence of the most important controls which, in the barter economy, keep the extension of the productive apparatus within economically permissible limits. *Once we assume that, even at a single point, the pricing process fails to equilibrate supply and demand, so that over a more or less long period demand may be satisfied at prices at which the available supply is inadequate to meet total demand, then the march of economic events loses its determinateness and a range of indeterminateness appears, within which movements can originate leading away from equilibrium.* And it is rightly assumed, as we shall see later on, that it is precisely the behaviour of interest, the price of credit, which makes possible these disturbances in price formation. We must not, however, overlook the fact that the range of

87

indeterminateness thus created is 'indeterminate' only in relation to the absolute determinateness of barter economy. The new price formation, together with the new structure of production determined by it, must in turn conform to certain laws, and the apparent indeterminateness does not imply unfettered mobility of prices and production. On the contrary, *every departure from the original equilibrium position is definitely determined by the new conditioning factor*. But if it is the existence of credit which makes these various disturbances possible, and if the volume and direction of new credits determines the extent of deviations from the equilibrium position, it is clearly not permissible to regard credit as a kind of passive element, and its presence as a self-evident condition. One must regard it rather as the new determining factor whose appearance causes these deviations and whose effects must form our starting-point when deducing all those phenomena which can be observed in cyclical fluctuations. Only when we have succeeded in doing this can we claim to have explained the phenomena described.

The neglect to derive the appearance of disproportionality from this condition, which must be assumed in order to keep the argument within the framework of equilibrium theory, leads to certain consequences which are best exemplified in the work of Professor Spiethoff. For, in his theory, all important interconnections are worked out in the fullest detail and none of the observed phenomena remains unaccounted for. But he is not able to deduce the various phenomena described from the single factor which, by virtue of its role in disturbing the inter-relationships of general equilibrium, should form the basis of his explanation. At each stage of his exposition he calls in experience to back him up and to show what deviations from the equilibrium position actually occur within the given range of indeterminateness. Consequently it never becomes clear why these phenomena *must* always occur as they are described; and there always remains a possibility that, on some other occasion, they may occur in a different way, or in a different order, without his being able to account for this difference on the basis of his exposition. In other words the latter, however accurately and pertinently it describes the observed phenomena, does not qualify as a theory in the rigid sense of the word, for it does not set out those conditions in whose presence events *must* follow a scientifically determined course.

IX

Although there is no doubt that all non-monetary Trade Cycle theories tacitly assume that the production of capital goods has been made possible by the creation of new credit, and although this condition is often emphasized in the course of the exposition,* no one has yet proved that this circumstance should form the exclusive basis of the explanation. As far as strict logic is concerned, it would not be impossible for such theories to make use of some other assumption which is capable of dissolving the rigid inter-relationships of equilibrium and, therefore, of forming the basis of an exact theoretical analysis. But once we assume the existence of credit in our

* Cf. Spiethoff, *op. cit.*, pp. 77–78 and 81.

explanation, we can attack the problem by seeing how far the objections which were raised earlier against the validity of the various theories under a barter economy are invalidated when the new assumption is made. Then we shall also be able to determine whether this assumption has necessarily to be made in the usual form, or whether it only represents a special instance of a far more widely significant extension of the assumptions of elementary theory.

The question we have to ask ourselves is: What new price-determining factor is introduced by the assumption of a credit supply which can be enlarged while other conditions remain unchanged — a factor capable of deflecting the tendency towards the establishment of equilibrium between supply and demand? Whether we necessarily accept that answer which, to my mind, is the only possible one depends on whether we agree with a certain basic proposition, which could only be briefly outlined here and whose full proof could only be given within the framework of a complete system of pure economics; namely, the proposition that, in a barter economy, interest

forms a sufficient regulator for the proportional development of the production of capital goods and consumption goods, respectively. If it is admitted that, in the absence of money, interest would effectively prevent any excessive extension of the production of production goods, by keeping it within the limits of the available supply of savings, and that an extension of the stock of capital goods which is based on a voluntary postponement of consumers' demand into the future can never lead to disproportionate extensions, then it must also necessarily be admitted that disproportional developments in the production of capital goods can arise only through the independence of the supply of free money capital from the accumulation of savings; which in turn arises from the elasticity of the volume of money.*
Every change in the volume of means of circulation is, in fact, an event to be distinguished

> ˎ * 'Volume of money', in this connection, does not mean merely the quantity of money in circulation but the volume of the money stream or the effective circulation (in the usual terminology — quantity *times* velocity of circulation). Even so, certain changes in the effective circulation may have no disturbing effect because of certain compensating changes in business organization. On this point see my *Prices and Production*, Lecture IV.

from all other real causes, for the purpose of
theoretical reasoning; for, unlike all others, it
implies a loosening of the inter-relationships of
equilibrium. No change in 'real' factors, whether
in the amount of available means of production,
in consumers' preferences, or elsewhere, can do
away with that final identity of total demand and
total supply on which every conception of economic equilibrium is based. A change in the volume
of money, on the other hand, represents as it were
a one-sided change in demand, which is not
counterbalanced by an equivalent change in supply.
Money, being a pure means of exchange, not being
wanted by anyone for purposes of consumption,
must by its nature always be re-exchanged without ever having entirely fulfilled its purpose; thus
when it is present it loosens that finality and
'closedness' of the system which is the fundamental assumption of static theory, and leads to
phenomena which the closed system of static
equilibrium renders inconceivable.*

* This dissolution of the 'closedness' of the system, arising because
a change in the volume of money is a one-sided change in demand
unaccompanied by an equivalent change in supply, does not mean of
course that Löwe's plea for an 'open' system ("Wie ist Konjunktur-

Together with the 'closedness' of the system there necessarily disappears the interdependence of all its parts, and thus prices become possible which do not operate according to the self-regulating principles of the economic system described by static theory. On the contrary, these prices may elicit movements which not only do not lead to a new equilibrium position but which actually create new disturbances of equilibrium. In this way, through the inclusion of money among the basic assumptions of exposition, it becomes possible to deduce *a priori* phenomena such as those observed in cyclical fluctuations. One instance of these disturbances in the price mechanism, brought about by monetary influences — and the one which is most important from the point of view of Trade Cycle theory — is that putting out of action of the 'interest brake' which is taken for granted by the Trade Cycle theories examined above. How far this circumstance forms a suffi-

theorie überhaupt möglich') has been granted. (Löwe thinks of a system when one or several 'independent variables' are drawn in for explanation.) This plea, which one is tempted to believe has been dictated by a desire to free theory from the trammels of exact deduction, has been justly and strongly criticized by E. Carell (*op. cit.* pp. 2 *et seq.* and 115).

cient basis for a theory of the Trade Cycle is a problem of the concrete elaboration of monetary explanation, and will, therefore, be dealt with in the next chapter, where we shall examine how far existing monetary theories have already tackled those problems which are relevant to a theory of the Trade Cycle.

X

The purpose of the foregoing chapter was to show that only the assumption of primary monetary changes can fulfil the fundamentally necessary condition of any theoretical explanation of cyclical fluctuations — a condition which is not fulfilled by any theory based exclusively on 'real' processes. If this is true then, at the outset of theoretical exposition, those monetary processes must be recognized as decisive causes. *For we can gain a theoretically unexceptionable explanation of complex phenomena only by first assuming the full activity of the elementary economic interconnections as shown by the equilibrium theory, and then introducing, consciously and successively, just those*

95

elements which are capable of relaxing these rigid inter-relationships. All the phenomena which become possible only as a result of this relaxation must then be explained — as consequences of the particular elements, through whose inclusion among the elementary assumptions they become explicable within the framework of general theory. In place of such a theoretical deduction, we often find an assertion, unfounded on any system, of a far-reaching indeterminacy in the economy. Paradoxically stated as it is, this thesis is bound to have a devastating effect on theory; for it involves the sacrifice of any exact theoretical deduction, and the very possibility of a theoretical explanation of economic phenomena is rendered problematic.

Similar objections of a general nature must be levelled against another large group of theories which we have not yet mentioned. This group pays close attention to the monetary inter-connections and expressly emphasizes them as a necessary condition for the occurrence of the processes described. But they fail to pass from this realization to the necessary conclusion; to make it a starting-point for their theoretical elaboration, from which all other particular phenomena have to be deduced. To this group belongs the theory of Professor J. Schumpeter, and certain 'under-consumption theories'* notably that of Professor E. Lederer; and, similarly, the various 'realistic' theories — that is, those which renounce any unified theoretical deduction, such as those of Professors G. Cassel, J. Lescure and Wesley Mitchell. With regard to all these semi-monetary explanations, we must ask whether — once we have been compelled to introduce new assumptions foreign to the static system — it is not the first task of a theoretical investigation to examine all the consequences which must necessarily ensue from this new assumption, and, in so far as any phenomena are thus proved to be logically derivable from the latter, to regard them in the course of the exposition as effects of the new condition introduced. Only in this way is it possible to incorporate Trade Cycle theory into

* For a detailed criticism of a representative specimen of modern under-consumption theories, that of Messrs. W. T. Foster and W. Catchings, see my article on The 'Paradox' of Saving, 'Economica' No. 32, May 1931.

97

the static system which is the basis of all theoretical economics; and, for this very reason, the monetary elements must be regarded as decisive factors in the explanation of cyclical fluctuations. The contrast therefore can be reduced to a question of theoretical presentation, and it may even seem, when comparing these theories, that the matter of the express recognition of the monetary starting-point is one of purely methodological or even terminological importance, having no bearing on the essential solution of the problem. But the same procedure which in one case may only lead to a lapse from theoretical elegance, breaking the unity of the theoretical structure, may in another case lead to the introduction of thoroughly faulty reasoning, against which only a rigid systematical procedure provides an effective security.

MONETARY THEORIES OF THE TRADE CYCLE

CHAPTER III

MONETARY THEORIES OF THE TRADE CYCLE

I

THE argument of the foregoing chapters has demonstrated the main reason for the necessity of the monetary approach to Trade Cycle theory. It arises from the circumstance that the automatic adjustment of supply and demand can only be disturbed when money is introduced into the economic system. This adjustment must be considered, according to the reasoning which it most clearly expressed in Say's *Théorie des Débouchés*, as being always present in a state of natural economy. Every explanation of the Trade Cycle which uses the methods of economic theory — which of course is only possible through systematic co-ordination of the former with the fundamental propositions of the latter -- must, therefore, start by considering the influences which emanate from the use of money. By following up their results it should be possible to demonstrate the total effect on the economic system, and formulate the result into a co-ordinated whole. This must be the aim of all theories which set out to explain disturbances in equilibrium which, by their very nature, cannot be regarded as immediate consequences of changes in data, but only as arising out of the development of the economic system itself. For that typical form of disturbance, which experience shows to be regularly recurrent and which can properly be called the Trade Cycle, the influence of money should be sought in the fact that when the volume of money is elastic, there may exist a lack of rigidity in the relationship between saving and the creation of real capital. This is a fact which nearly all the theories of the disproportional production of capital goods are agreed in emphasizing. It is, therefore, the first task of monetary Trade Cycle theory to show why, and how, monetary influences directly bring about regular disturbances in just this part of the economic system.

I I

Naturally no attempt will be made at this stage to present such a theory systematically. This chapter is concerned with one particular task: it attempts to show how far existing monetary theories have already gone towards a satisfactory solution of the problem of the Trade Cycle, and what corrections are needed in order to invalidate certain objections which, up to the present, have appeared well founded.

It should already be clear that what we expect from a monetary Trade Cycle theory differs considerably from what most of the monetary Trade Cycle theories regard as the essential aim of their explanation. We are in no way concerned to explain the effect of the monetary factor on trade fluctuations through changes in the value of money and variations in the price level — subjects which form the main basis of current monetary theories. We expect such an explanation to emerge rather from a study of all the changes originating in the monetary field — more especially variations in its quantity — changes which are bound to disturb the equilibrium inter-relationships existing in the natural economy, *whether the disturbance shows itself in a change in the so-called 'general value of money' or not*. Our plea for a monetary approach to all Trade Cycle theory does not, therefore, imply that henceforward such theories should be exclusively, or even principally, based on those arguments which usually predominate in writings on money, and which set out to explain the general level of prices and alterations in the 'value of money'. On the contrary, monetary theory should not merely be concerned with money for its own sake, but should also study those phenomena which distinguish the money economy from the equilibrium inter-relationships of barter economy which must always be assumed by 'pure economics'.

It must of course be admitted that many Trade Cycle theorists regard the importance of monetary theory as residing precisely in its ability to explain the cause of fluctuations by reference to changes in the general price level. Hence, it is not difficult to understand why certain economists believe that, once they have rejected this view, they have settled once and for all with the monetary explanations of the Trade Cycle. It is not surprising that monetary theories of the Trade Cycle should be rejected by those who, like Professor A. Spiethoff in his well-known work on the Quantity Theory as *'Haussetheorie'*,* identify them with the naive quantity-theory explanations which derive fluctuations from changes in the price-level.† Against such a conception it can rightly be urged that there are a number of phenomena tending to bring about fluctuations, which certainly do not depend on changes in the value of money, and which can, in fact, exert a disturbing effect on the economic equilibrium without these changes occurring at all. Again, in spite of many assertions to the contrary, fluctuations in the

---

* 'Die Quantitätstheorie, insbesondere in ihrer Verwertbarkeit als Haussetheorie'. Festgaben für A. Wagner zur 70 Wiederkehr seines Geburtstages, Leipzig, 1905, pp. 299 *et seq.*

† F. Burchardt, A. Löwe, and other more recent critics of monetary trade cycle theory, also fall within this category. They recognize no other kind of monetary influence than that which manifests itself through changes in the price-level; and as a result of this undoubtedly false conception they quite definitely conclude that there can be no such thing as pure monetary trade cycle theory. In their view the theories which are usually so called nearly always depend, in fact, on what they regard as non-monetary factors.

general price-level need not always be ascribed to monetary causes.*

III

But theories which explain the Trade Cycle in terms of fluctuations in the general price-level must be rejected not only because they fail to show why the monetary factor disturbs the general equilibrium, but also because their fundamental hypothesis is, from a theoretical standpoint, every bit as naive as that of those theories which entirely neglect the influence of money. They start off with a 'normal position' which, however, has nothing to do with the normal position obtaining in the static state; and they are based on a postulate, the postulate of a constant

* The assertion that changes in the *general* level of prices must always originate on the monetary side, as is argued for example by Professors G. Cassel and Irving Fisher, obviously depends on circular reasoning. It starts from the postulate that the amount of money must be adjusted to changes in the volume of trade in such a way that the price-level shall remain unchanged. *If it is not, and the volume of money remains unaltered, then,* according to this remarkable argument, *the latter becomes the cause* (!) of changes in the price level. This statement is made quite baldly by Professor G. Cassel in his book *Money and Foreign Exchange After* 1914. London, 1922.

price-level, which, if fulfilled, suffices in itself to break down the inter-relationships of equilibrium. All these theories, indeed, are based on the idea — quite groundless but hitherto virtually unchallenged — that if only the value of money does not change it ceases to exert a direct and independent influence on the economic system. But this assumption (which is present, more or less, in the work of all monetary theorists), so far from being the necessary starting-point for all trade cycle theory, is perhaps the greatest existing hindrance to a successful examination of the course of cyclical fluctuations. It forces us to assume variations in the effective quantity of money as given. Such variations, however, always dissolve the equilibrium inter-relationships described by static theory; but they must necessarily be assumed if the value of money is to remain constant despite changes in data; and therefore they cannot be used to explain deviations from the course of events which static theory lays down. The only proper starting-point for any explanation based on equilibrium theory must be the effect of a change in the volume of money; for this, in itself, constitutes a new state of affairs, entirely different from that generally treated within the framework of static theory.

In complete contrast to those economic changes conditioned by 'real' forces, influencing simultaneously total supply and total demand, changes in the volume of money have, so to speak, a one-sided influence which elicits no reciprocal adjustment in the economic activity of different individuals. By deflecting a single factor, without simultaneously eliciting corresponding changes in other parts of the system, it dissolves its 'closedness', makes a breach in the rigid reaction mechanism of the system (which rests on the ultimate identity of supply and demand) and opens a way for tendencies leading away from the equilibrium position. As a theory of these one-sided influences, the theory of monetary economy should, therefore, be able to explain the occurrence of phenomena which would be inconceivable in the barter economy, and notably the disproportional developments which give rise to crises.* A starting-

* F. Wieser in *Der Geldwert und seine geschichtlichen Veränderungen* (Zeitschrift für Volkswirtschaft Sozialpolitik und Verwaltung, vol. xiii, 1907, p. 57, reprinted in F. Wieser, *Abhandlungen;* Tübingen, 1929, p. 178) has dealt with the special effects of a 'one-sided money supply'.

point for such explanations should be found in the possibility of alterations in the quantity of money occurring automatically and in the normal course of events, under the present organization of money and credit, without the need for violent or artificial action by any external agency.

IV

Even if a systematic treatment of the Trade Cycle problem has not yet been forthcoming, it should be noted that, throughout the different attempts at monetary explanation, there runs a secondary idea which is closely allied to that of the direct dependence of fluctuations on changes in the value of money. It is true that this idea is used merely as a subordinate device of technique to assist in the explanation of fluctuations in the value of money. But its development included the analysis of the most important elements in the monetary factors chiefly connected with the Trade Cycle. This was done in the teaching which began with H. Thornton*

* *An Enquiry into the Nature and Effects of the Paper Credit of Great Britain*, London, 1802; especially pp. 287 *et seq*. This is

and D. Ricardo* and was taken up again by
H. D. Macleod,† H. Sidgwick, R. Giffen and
J. S. Nicholson,‡ and finally developed by A.
Marshall,§ K. Wicksell,‖ and L. v. Mises,¶

one of the most remarkable accomplishments in monetary theory,
and still commands great attention; cf. the references to it by K.
Wicksell in the preface to the second volume of his *Vorlesungen
über Nationalökonomie auf Grundlage des Marginalprinzipes*, Jena,
1922, p. xii; and Burchardt, *op. cit.* For a fuller discussion of these
earlier theories, see my 'Prices and Production,' London, 1931, p. 11ff.

* Cf. 'The high price of bullion' (*Essays*, Gonner edit., p. 35),
where Ricardo says that 'interest would, during that interval be
under its natural level,' and also Chapter XXVII of his *Principles*
(McCulloch ed., p. 220), which for a long time have passed almost
unnoticed but which already contained much of what is set out in
later theories.

† *Theory and Practice of Banking*, 1855 and later editions. See
particularly vol. ii, pp. 278 *et seq.*

‡ For H. Sidgwick, R. Giffen and J. S. Nicholson, cf. J. W. Angell's
Theory of International Prices-History, Criticism and Restatement,
Cambridge, 1926, pp. 117–122.

§ Cf. his evidence before the various Parliamentary Commissions
which is collected in the volume *Official Papers by Alfred Marshall*,
London, 1926, especially pp. 38-41, 45, 46 *et seq.* 273 *et seq.*, as
well as the later account in 'Money, Credit, and Commerce,' pp.
255-56.

‖ Especially in *Geldzins und Güterpreise*, Jena, 1898, as well
as in the second volume of his later *Vorlesungen*, already quoted,
which has not had the influence which it deserved, mainly on account
of the exceedingly bad German translation in which it appeared.
I had unfortunately no means of access to the other Swedish works
connected with that of Wicksell, which should certainly not be
overlooked if one is to achieve a complete survey of the development
of this theory.

¶ *Theorie des Geldes und der Umlaufsmittel*, 1st edit. 1912, 2nd

whose works trace the development of the effects
on the structure of production of a rate of interest
which alters relatively to the equilibrium rate,
as a result of monetary influences. For the
purpose of this review it is unnecessary to go
back to the earlier representatives of this group;
it is enough to consider the conceptions of Wicksell
and Mises, since both the recent improvements
which have been effected and the errors which
still subsist can be best examined on the basis
of these studies.*

It must be taken for granted that the reader is
acquainted with the works of both Wicksell and
Mises. Wicksell, from the outset,† regards the
problem as concerning explicitly the *average*
change in the price of goods which from the

edit. 1924; also the more recent *Geldwertstabilisierung und Konjunk-turpolitik*, Jena, 1928. [A translation of the former will shortly appear in the present series. Ed.]

* Professor A. Hahn, whose views regarding trade cycle theory (put forward in *Volkswirtschaftlichen Theorie des Bankkredits*, Tübingen, 1920) are in some respects similar to those of Professor Mises, cannot be considered here, since we are unable to follow him in all those points in which he differs from the latter. Similar theories have also been put forward quite recently by Professor W. Röpke and S. Budge.

† See e.g. *Geldzins und Güterpreise*, p. 125.

theoretical standpoint is quite irrelevant. He starts from the hypothesis that, in the absence of disturbing monetary influences, the average price-level must remain unchanged. This assumption is based on another, only incidentally expressed,* which is not worked out and which, from the point of view of most of the problems dealt with, is not even permissible; i.e. the assumption of a stationary state of the economy. His fundamental thesis is that when the money rate of interest coincides with the natural rate (i.e. that rate which exactly balances the demand for loan capital and the supply of savings)† then money bears a completely *neutral* relationship to the price of goods, and tends neither to raise nor to lower it. But, owing to the nature of his basic assumptions, this thesis enables him to show deductively only that every lag of the money-rate behind the natural rate must lead to a rise in the general price-level, and every increase of the money-rate above the natural rate to a fall in general price-level. It is only incidentally, in the course of his

* Ibid., p. 126.
† Ibid., p. 93 and also *Vorlesungen*, vol. ii, p. 220.

analysis of the effects on the price-level of a money rate of interest differing from the natural rate that Wicksell touches on the consequences of such a distortion of the natural price formation (made possible by elasticity in the volume of currency) on the development of particular branches of production; and it is this question which is of the most decisive importance to Trade Cycle theory. If one were to make a systematic attempt to co-ordinate these ideas into an explanation of the Trade Cycle (dropping, as is essential, the assumption of the stationary state) a curious contradiction would arise. On the one hand, we are told that *the price level remains unaltered when the money-rate of interest is the same as the natural rate*; and, on the other, that *the production of capital goods is, at the same time, kept within the limits imposed by the supply of real savings*. One need say no more in order to show that there are cases — certainly all cases of an expanding economy, which are those most relevant to Trade Cycle theory — in which the rate of interest which equilibrates the supply of real savings and the demand for capital cannot be the rate of interest which also prevents changes in the price-level.* In this case, stability of the price-level presupposes changes in the volume of money: but these changes must always lead to a discrepancy between the amount of real savings and the volume of investment. *The rate of interest at which, in an expanding economy, the amount of new money entering circulation is just sufficient to keep the price-level stable, is always lower than the rate which would keep the amount of available loan-capital equal to the amount simultaneously saved by the public*: and thus, despite the stability of the price-level, it makes possible a development leading away from the equilibrium position. But Wicksell does not recognize here a monetary influence tending, independently of changes in the price-level, to break down the equilibrium system of barter economics: so long as the stability of the price level is undisturbed, everything appears to him to be in order.† Obsessed by the notion that the only aim of monetary theory is to explain

* Similarly also W. Eucken, *op. cit.* pp. 300 *et seq.*
† Wicksell's justification of this view in *Geldzins und Güterpreise* (see p. 97) is incomprehensible to me.

those phenomena which cause the value of money to alter, he thinks himself justified in neglecting all deviations of the processes of money-economy from those of barter-economy, so long as they throw no direct light on the determination of the value of money: and thus he shuts the door on the possibility of a general theory covering all the consequences of the phenomena which he indicates.* But although his thesis of a direct relationship between movements in the price-level and deviations of the money-rate of interest from

* R. Stucken in his *Theorie der Konjunkturschwankungen* (Jena, 1926, p. 26) was one of the first to draw attention to the fact that the relation, indicated by Wicksell, between a money rate of interest diverging from the natural rate, and movements in the price-level only exists in a stationary economy; while, if the flow of goods is increasing, only an addition to purchasing power can secure stability in the price-level. He remains, however, entirely steeped in the prevalent opinion that a stable price-level is indispensable to undisturbed economic development, and therefore holds that the additional money necessary to secure that condition cannot be regarded as an element of disturbance in the economic process. Similarly Mr. D. H. Robertson pointed out at about the same time (*Banking Policy and the Price Level*, London, 1926, p. 99) that the rate of interest which keeps the price-level stable need not coincide with that which equates the supply of savings with the demand for capital. I am now informed that, even before the war, this objection formed the basis of a criticism directed by Prof. David Davidson of Upsala against Wicksell's theory. Prof. Davidson's article and the subsequent discussion with Wicksell in the Swedish *Economisk Tidskrift* are, however, inaccessible to me.

its natural level, holds good only in a stationary state, and is therefore inadequate for an explanation of cyclical fluctuations, his account of the effects of this deviation on the price structure and the development of the various branches of production constitutes the most important basis for any future monetary Trade Cycle theory. But this future theory, unlike that of Wicksell, will have to examine not movements in the general price-level but rather those deviations of particular prices from their equilibrium position which were caused by the monetary factor.

V

The investigations of Professor Mises represent a big step forward in this direction, although he still regards the fluctuations in the value of money as the main object of his explanation, and deals with the phenomena of disproportionality only in so far as they can be regarded as consequences — in the widest sense of the term — of these fluctuations. But Professor Mises' conception of the intrinsic value of money extends the notion of 'fluctuations in money value' far beyond the limits of what this term is commonly under-stood to mean; and so he is in a position to describe within the framework, or rather under the name, of a theory of fluctuations in the value of money, all monetary influences on price formation.* His exposition already contains an account of practically all those effects of a rate of interest altered through monetary influences, which are

* If one follows C. Menger and now Professor Mises in disregarding ordinary usage and including in the theory of the value of money *all* influences of money on prices, instead of restricting it to an explana-tion of the general purchasing power of money (by which is understood the absolute level of money prices as distinct from the relative prices of particular goods) then it is correct to say that any economic theory of money must be a theory of the value of money. But this use of the phrase is hardly opportune, for 'value of money' is usually taken to mean 'general purchasing power', while *monetary theory has by no means finished its work when it has explained the absolute level of prices (or, as Wicksell would call it, the 'concrete' level); its far more important task is to explain those changes in the relative height of particular prices which are conditioned by the introduction of money.* On the other hand, to avoid any possible misunderstanding we must particularly insist at this point that in the sense of the famous contrast between such nominalistic theories as the 'state theory' of Knapp, and the catallactic theories in general, the monetary theory which we are seeking will also have to be exclusively a 'theory of money values'. In justice to Menger and Mises, it should be pointed out that what they mean when they speak of the stability of the 'inner' value of money, has nothing to do with any measurable value, in the sense of some price level; but is only another and, as it seems to me, misleading, expression for what I now prefer to call neutrality of money. (Cf. my *Prices and Produc-*

important for an explanation of the course of the Trade Cycle. Thus he describes the disproportionate development of various branches of production and the resulting changes in the income structure. And yet this presentation of his theory under the guise of a theory of fluctuation in the value of money remains dangerous, partly because it always gives rise to misunderstandings, but mainly because it seems to bring into the foreground a secondary effect of cyclical fluctuations, an effect which generally accompanies the latter but which need not necessarily do so.

This is no place to examine the extent to which Professor Mises escapes from this difficulty by using the concept of the inner objective value of money. For us, the only point of importance is that the effects of an artificially lowered rate of interest, pointed out by Wicksell and Mises, exist

tion, pp. 27-28 and *passim*). This expression, first used by Wicksell in the passage quoted earlier in the text, has of late become fairly common in German and Dutch writings on money. Cf. L. v. Bortkiewicz, *Die Frage der Reform unserer Währung*, Brauns Analen, vol. vi, 1919, pp. 57-59; W. G. Behrens, *Das Geldschöpfungsproblem*, Jena, 1928, pp. 228 *et seq.*, 286 and 312; G. M. Verrijin Stuart and J. G. Koopmans in the reports and discussions of the 1929 meeting of the 'Vereinigung voor de Staathuishoudkunde en de Statistik'.

whether this same circumstance does or does not eventually react on the general value of money, in the sense of its purchasing power. Therefore they must be dealt with independently if they are to be properly understood.* Increases in the volume of circulation, which in an expanding economy serve to prevent a drop in the price-level, present a typical instance of a change in the monetary factor calculated to cause a discrepancy between the money and natural rate of interest without affecting the price-level These changes are consequently neglected, as a rule, in dealing with phenomena of disproportionality; but they are bound to lead to a distribution of productive resources between capital-goods and consumption-goods which differs from the equilibrium distribution, just as those changes in the monetary factor which do manifest themselves in changes in the price-level. This case is particularly important, because under contemporary currency

* Professor Mises recently admitted this, in principle, when he explicitly emphasized the fact that *every* new issue of circulating media brings about a lowering of the money rate of interest in relation to the natural rate. (*Geldwertstabilisierung und Konjunkturpolitik*, p. 57.)

systems the automatic adjustment of the value of money, in the form of a flow of precious metals, will regularly make available new supplies of purchasing power which will depress the money-rate of interest below its natural level.*

Since a stable price-level has been regarded as normal hitherto, far too little investigation has been made into the effects of these changes in the volume of money, which necessarily cause a development different from that which would be expected on the basis of static theory, and which lead to the establishment of a structure of production incapable of perpetuating itself once the change in the monetary factor has ceased to operate. Economists have overlooked the fact that the changes in the volume of money, which, in an expanding economy, are necessary to maintain price stability, lead to a new state of affairs foreign to static analysis, so that the development which occurs under a stable price level cannot be regarded as consonant with static

* Cf. also my article, 'Das intertemporale Gleichgewichtssystem der Preise und die Bewegungen des Geldwertes', Weltwirtschaftliches Archiv, vol. 28, July 1928.

laws. Thus the disturbances described as resulting from changes in the *value* of money form only a small part of the much wider category of deviations from the static course of events brought about by changes in the *volume* of money — which may often exist without changes in the value of money, while they may also fail to accompany changes in value of money when the latter occur.

V I

As has been briefly indicated above, most of the objections raised against monetary theories of cyclical fluctuations rest on the mistaken idea that their significant contribution consists in deducing changes in the volume of production from the movement of prices *en bloc*. In particular, the very extensive criticism recently levelled by Dr. Burchardt and Professor Löwe against monetary Trade Cycle theory is based throughout on the idea that this theory must start from the wave-like fluctuations of the price-level, which are conditioned mainly by monetary causes; the rise, as well as the fall, of the price-level being brought about by particular new forces originating on the side of money. It is only through this special assumption, which is also stated explicitly, that Professor Löwe's systematic presentation of his objections in his latest work* becomes comprehensible; he is completely misleading when he asserts that, if it is to raise the monetary factor to the rank of a *conditio sine qua non* of the Trade Cycle, monetary theory ought to prove that the effectiveness of all non-monetary factors depends on a previous price-boom.† We have already shown that it is not even necessary, in order to ascribe the cause of cyclical fluctuations to monetary changes, to assume that these monetary causes act through changes in the general price-level. It is therefore impossible to maintain that the importance of monetary theories lies solely in an explanation of price cycles.‡

But even the essential point in the criticism of Löwe and Burchardt—the assertion that all monetary theories explain the transition from boom to

---

* *Uber den Einfluss monetärer Faktoren auf den Konjunkturzyklus*, *op. cit.* pp. 361-368.

† *Op. cit.* p. 366.

‡ As is maintained by Professor Löwe (*op. cit.*, p. 364).

depression not in terms of monetary causes but in terms of other causes super-added to the monetary explanation—rests exclusively on the idea that only general price changes can be recognized as monetary effects. But general price changes are no essential feature of a monetary theory of the Trade Cycle; *they are not only unessential, but they would be completely irrelevant if only they were completely 'general' — that is, if they affected all prices at the same time and in the same proportion.* The point of real interest to Trade Cycle theory is the existence of certain deviations in individual price-relations occurring because changes in the volume of money appear at certain individual points; deviations, that is, away from the position which is necessary to maintain the whole system in equilibrium. Every disturbance of the equilibrium of prices leads *necessarily* to shifts in the structure of production, which must therefore be regarded as consequences of monetary change, never as additional separate assumptions. The nature of the changes in the composition of the existing stock of goods, which are effected through such monetary changes, depends of course on the point at which the money is injected into the economic system.

There is no doubt that the emphasis placed on this phenomenon marks the most important advance made by monetary science beyond the elementary truths of the quantity theory. Monetary theory no longer rests content with determining the final reaction of a given monetary cause on the purchasing power of money, but attempts instead to trace the successive alterations in particular prices, which eventually bring about a change in the whole price system.* The assumption of a 'time lag' between the successive changes in various prices has not been spun out of thin air solely for the purposes of Trade Cycle theory; it is a correction, based on systematic reasoning, of the mistaken conceptions of older monetary theories.† Of course, the expression 'time lag,'

---

* On the development of this point of view, see **Chap.** 1 of my *Prices and Production*.

† We cannot, therefore, regard Mises' pronouncement at the Zürich debate of the Verein für Sozialpolitik as a surrender of the monetary standpoint. On this occasion, he not only admitted but indeed emphasized the fact that monetary causes can only act by producing a 'lag' between various prices, wages and interest rates. (Cf. *Verhandlungen des Vereins für Sozialpolitik in Zürich*, Schriften des Vereins, vol. 175, München and Leipzig, 1929.)

borrowed from Anglo-American writers and deno-
ting a temporary lagging behind of the changes
in the price of some goods relatively to the
changes in the price of other goods, is a very
unsuitable expression when the shifts in relative
prices are due to changes in demand which are
themselves conditioned by monetary changes. For
such shifts are bound to continue so long as the
change in demand persists. They disappear only
with the disappearance of the disturbing monetary
factor. They cease when money ceases to
increase or diminish further, *not*, however,
when the increase or diminution has itself been
wiped out. But, whatever expression we may use
to denote these changes in relative prices and the
changes in the structure of production conditioned
by them, there can be no doubt that they are, in
turn, conditioned by monetary causes, which
alone make them possible.

The only plausible objection to this argument
would be that the shifts in price-relationships
occurring at any point in the economic system
could not possibly cause those typical, regularly
recurring, shifts in the structure of production

which we observe in cyclical fluctuations. In opposition to this view, as we shall show in more detail later, it can be urged that those changes which are constantly taking place in our money and credit organization cause a certain price, the rate of interest, to deviate from the equilibrium position, and that deviations of this kind *necessarily* lead to such changes in the relative position of the various branches of production as are bound later to precipitate the crisis.* There is one important point, however, which must be emphasized against the above-named critics; namely, that it is not only when the crisis is directly occasioned by a new monetary factor, separate from that which originally brought about the boom, that it is to be regarded as conditioned by monetary causes. Once the monetary causes have brought about that development in the whole

---

* It is not essential, as Burchardt maintains (*op. cit.*, p. 124) to base this analysis on any particular theory of interest, such as that of Böhm-Bawerk; it is equally consonant with all modern interest theories. The reason why, under the circumstances assumed, interest fails to equilibrate production for the future and production for the present, is bound up not with the special form in which interest in general is explained, but with the deviations, due to monetary causes, of the current rate of interest from the equilibrium rate.

economic system which is known as a boom, sufficient forces have already been set in motion to ensure that, sooner or later, when the monetary influence has ceased to operate, a crisis must occur. The 'cause' of the crisis is, then, the disequilibrium of the whole economy occasioned by monetary changes and maintained through a longer period, possibly, by a succession of further monetary changes — a disequilibrium the origin of which can only be explained by monetary disturbances.

Professor Löwe's most important argument against the monetary theory of the Trade Cycle — an argument which so far as most existing monetary theories are concerned is unquestionably valid — will be discussed in more detail later. The sole purpose of the next chapter of this book is to show that the cycle is not only due to 'mistaken measures by monopolistic bodies' (as Professor Löwe assumes),* but that the reason for its continuous recurrence lies in an 'immanent necessity of the monetary and credit mechanism.'

* *Op. cit.*, p. 365 *et seq.*

VII

Among the phenomena which are fundamentally independent of changes in the value of
money, we must include, first of all, the effects of
a rate of interest lowered by monetary influences,
which must necessarily lead to the excessive
production of capital goods. Wicksell and Mises
both rightly emphasize the decisive importance
of this factor in the explanation of cyclical phenomena, as its effect will occur even when the
increase in circulation is only just sufficient to
prevent a fall in the price level. Besides this,
there exist a number of other phenomena, by
virtue of which a money economy (in the sense
of an economy with a variable money supply)
differs from a static economy, which for this
reason are important for a true understanding
of the course of the Trade Cycle. They have been
partly described already by Mises, but they can
only be clearly observed by taking as the central
subject of investigation not changes in general
prices but the divergences of the relation of
particular prices as compared with the price

system of static equilibrium. Phenomena of this sort include the changes in the relation of costs and selling prices and the consequent fluctuations in profits, which Professors Mitchell and Lescure in particular have made the starting point of their exposition; and the shifts in the distribution of incomes which Professor Lederer investigates — both of these phenomena depending for their explanation on monetary factors,* while neither of them can be immediately connected with changes in the general value of money. It is, perhaps, for this very reason that their authors, although perfectly realizing the monetary origin of the phenomena which they described, did not present their views as monetary theories. While we cannot attempt here to show the position which these phenomena would occupy in a systematically developed Trade Cycle theory (a task which really involves the development of a new theory, and which is unnecessary for the purposes of our present argument) it is not difficult to see

---

* That Professor Lederer himself sees this clearly is evident from his analysis, mentioned earlier, contained in the Grundriss der Sozialökonomik, vol. iv, part 1, pp. 390–91.

that all of them can be logically deduced from an initiating monetary disturbance,* which, in any case, we are compelled to assume in studying them. The special advantages of the monetary approach consist precisely in the fact that, by starting from a monetary disturbance, we are able to explain deductively all the different peculiarities observed in the course of the Trade Cycle, and so to protect ourselves against objections such as were raised in an earlier chapter against non-monetary theories. It makes it possible to look upon empirically recognized interconnections, which would otherwise rival one another as independent clues to an explanation, as necessary consequences of one common cause.

Much theoretical work will have to be done before such a theoretical system can be worked out in such detail that all the empirically observed characteristics of the Trade Cycle can find their explanation within its framework. Up to now, the monetary theories have unduly narrowed the field of phenomena to be explained, by limiting research

* Cf. Mises' presentation of the social effects of changes in the value of money: *Theorie des Geldes und der Umlaufsmittel*, pp. 178-200.

to those monetary changes which find their expression in changes in the general value of money. Thus they are prevented from showing the deviations of a money economy from a static economy in all their multiplicity. The problem of cyclical fluctuations can only be solved satisfactorily when a theory of the money economy itself — still almost entirely lacking at present — has been evolved, comprising a detailed discussion of all those points in which it differs from the equilibrium analysis worked out on the assumption of a pure barter economy. The full elaboration of this intermediate step of theoretical exposition is indispensable before we can achieve a Trade Cycle theory, which — as Böhm-Bawerk has expressed it in a phrase, often quoted but hardly ever taken to heart — must constitute the last chapter of the complete theory of social economy.* In my opinion, the most important step towards such a theory, which would embrace all new phenomena arising from the addition of money to the

* This expression occurs in connection with a review of E. v. Bergmann's *Geschichte der Nationalökonomischen Krisentheorien.* (Zeitschrift für Volkswirtschaft, Sozialpolitik und Verwaltung, vol. vii, 1898, p. 112.)

conditions assumed in elementary equilibrium theory, would be the emancipation of the theory of money from the restrictions which limit its scope to a discussion of the *value* of money.

VIII

Once, however, we have accomplished this urgently necessary displacement of the problem of monetary value from its present central position in monetary theory, we find ourselves in a position to come to an understanding with the most important non-monetary theorists of the Trade Cycle; for the effect of money on the 'real' economic processes will automatically be brought more to the surface, while monetary theory will no longer appear to be insisting on the immediate dependence of Trade Cycle phenomena on changes in the value of money — a claim which is certainly unjustified. On the other hand, a number of non-monetary theories do not question in the least the dependence of the processes which they describe on certain monetary assumptions; and in their case the only conflict now arising concerns the systematic presentation of these. It should be the task of our analysis to show that the placing of the monetary factor in the centre of the exposition is necessary in the interest of the unity of the system, and that the various 'real' interconnections, which, in certain theories, form the main basis of the explanation, can only find place in a closed system as consequences of the original monetary influences. There can hardly be any question, in the present state of research, as to what should be the basic idea of a completely developed theory of money. One can abandon those parts of the Wicksell-Mises theory which aim at explaining the movements in the general value of money, and develop to the full the effects of all discrepancies between the natural and money rates of interest on the relative development of the production of capital goods and consumption goods — a theory which has already been largely elaborated by Professor Mises. In this way, one can achieve, by purely deductive methods, the same picture of the process of cyclical fluctuations which the more realistic theories of Spiethoff and Cassel have al-

ready deduced from experience. Wicksell himself*
drew attention to the way in which the processes
deduced from his own theory harmonize with the
exposition of Spiethoff; and conversely, Spiethoff,
in a statement already quoted, has emphasized the
fact that the phenomena which he describes are all
conditioned by a change in monetary factors. But
it is only by placing monetary factors first that such
expositions as those of Spiethoff and Cassel can be
incorporated into the general system of theoretical
economics. A final point of decisive importance
is that the choice of the monetary starting point
enables us to deduce simultaneously all the other
phenomena, such as shifts in relative prices and
incomes, which are more empirically determined
and utilized as independent factors; and thus the
relations existing between them can be classified
and their relative position and importance determined within the framework of the theory.

* *Vorlesungen*, vol. ii, p. 238; Wicksell's review of Cassel's
textbook, which has since appeared in a German translation (Schmol-
lers Jahrbuch für Volkswirtschaft, Gesetzgebung und Verwaltung,
vol. 52, Munich, 1928), shows that, although he rightly opposes
Cassel's general system, he agrees to a large extent with his theory of
the Trade Cycle.

Even when these phenomena are, as yet, much further from a satisfactory explanation than are the disproportionalities in the development of production, which are cleared up in a greater degree, there can be no doubt that it will become possible to incorporate them also into a self-sufficient theory of the effects of monetary disturbances. These effects, however, although ultimately caused by monetary factors, do not fall within the narrower field of monetary theory. A well-developed theory of the Trade Cycle ought to deal thoroughly with them; but as this book is exclusively concerned with the monetary theories themselves, we shall, in the following chapters, only study the reasons why these monetary causes of the Trade Cycle inevitably recur under the existing system of money and credit organization, and what are the main problems with which future research is faced by reason of the realization of the determining role played by money.

THE FUNDAMENTAL CAUSE
OF CYCLICAL
FLUCTUATIONS

CHAPTER I

THE FUNDAMENTAL CAUSE OF CYCLICAL FLUCTUATIONS

I

So far we have not answered, or have only hinted at an answer to the question why, under the existing organization of the economic system, we constantly find those deviations of the money rate of interest from the equilibrium rate* which, as we have seen, must be regarded as the cause of the periodically recurring disproportionalities in the structure of production. The problem is, then, to discover the gap in the reaction mechanism of the modern economic system which is respon-

---

* The term 'equilibrium rate of interest' which, I believe, was introduced into Germany in this connection, by K. Schlesinger in his *Theorie der Geld-und Kreditwirtschaft* München and Leipzig, 1914, p. 128) seems to me preferable in this case to the usual expression of 'natural rate' or 'real rate.' Alfred Marshall used the term 'equilibrium level' as early as 1887 (cf. Official Papers of Alfred Marshall, p. 130). Cf. also chap. v. of the present work.

sible for the fact that certain changes of data, so far from being followed by a prompt readjustment (i.e. the formation of a new equilibrium) are, actually, the cause of recurrent shifts in economic activity which subsequently have to be reversed before a new equilibrium can be established.

The analysis of the foregoing chapters has shown that when it is possible to detect, in the organization of our economy, a dislocation in the reaction mechanism described by equilibrium theory, it should be possible (and should, indeed, be the object of a fully developed Trade Cycle theory) to describe deductively, as a necessary effect of the disturbance — quite apart from their observed occurrence — all the deviations in the course of economic events conditioned by this dislocation. It has been shown, in addition, that the primary cause of cyclical fluctuations must be sought in changes in the volume of money, which are undoubtedly always recurring and which, by their occurrence, always bring about a falsification of the pricing process, and thus a misdirection of production. The new element which we are seeking is, therefore, to be found in the 'elasticity' of the volume of money at the disposal of the economic system. It is this element whose presence forms the 'necessary and sufficient' condition for the emergence of the Trade Cycle.*

The question which we now have to examine is whether this elasticity in the volume of money is an immanent characteristic of our present money and credit system; whether, given certain conditions, changes in the volume of money and the resulting differences between the natural and the monetary rate of interest must necessarily occur, or whether they represent, so to speak, casual phenomena arising from arbitrary interferences by the authorities responsible for the regulation

---

* Mr. R. G. Hawtrey regards the following theses as important for monetary Trade Cycle theories: (1) That certain monetary and credit movements are necessary and sufficient conditions of the observed phenomena of the Trade Cycle; and (2) that the periodicity of those phenomena can be explained by purely monetary tendencies which cause the movements to take place successively and to be spread over a considerable period of years. ('The Monetary Theory of the Trade Cycle and its Statistical Test': *Quarterly Journal of Economics*, vol. 41, p. 472). This entirely correct definition of Mr. Hawtrey's should have prevented Dr. Burchardt and Prof. Löwe, who expressly fasten on this point in their criticism of monetary Trade Cycle theories, from looking from monetary influences to changes in the general value of money, while disregarding the changes in the distributive process which are conditioned by monetary causes.

of the volume of currency media. Is it an inherent necessity of the existing monetary and credit system that its reaction to certain changes in data is different from what we should expect on the basis of economic equilibrium theory; or are these discrepancies to be explained by special assumptions regarding the nature of the monetary administration, i.e. by a series of what might be called 'political' assumptions? The question whether the recurrence of credit cycles is, or is not, due to an unavoidable characteristic of the existing economic organization, depends on whether the existing monetary and credit organization in itself necessitates changes in the currency media, or whether these are brought about only by the special interference of external agencies. The answer to this question will also decide into which of the most commonly accepted categories a given Trade Cycle theory is to be placed. We must deal briefly with this point because a false classification, which is largely the fault of the exponents of the monetary theories, has contributed much to make them misunderstood.

I I

If we are to understand the present status
of monetary theories of the Trade Cycle, we must
pay special attention to the assumptions upon
which they are based. At the present day, monetary theories are generally regarded as falling
within the class of so-called 'exogenous' theories,
i.e. theories which look for the cause of the cycle
not in the interconnections of economic phenomena themselves but in external interferences.
Now it is, no doubt, often a waste of time to discuss
the merits of classifying a theory in a given category.
But the question of classification becomes important when the inclusion of a theory in one class
or another implies, at the same time, a judgment
as to the sphere of validity of the theory in
question. This is undoubtedly the case with the
distinction, very general to-day, between *endogenous* and *exogenous* theories — a distinction introduced into economic literature some twenty
years ago by Bouniatian.* Endogenous theories,

* *Studien zur Theorie und Geschichte der Wirtschaftskrisen*, Munich,
1908, p. 3.

in the course of their proof, avoid making use of assumptions which cannot either be decided by purely economic considerations, or regarded as general characteristics of our economic system — and hence capable of general proof. Exogenous theories, on the other hand, are based on concrete assertions whose correctness has to be proved separately in each individual case. As compared with an endogenous theory, which, if logically sound, can in a sense lay claim to general validity, an exogenous theory is at some disadvantage, inasmuch as it has, in each case, to justify the assumptions on which its conclusions are based.

Now as far as most contemporary monetary theories of the cycle are concerned, their opponents are undoubtedly right in classifying them, as does Professor Löwe* in his discussion of the theories of Professors Mises and Hahn, among the exogenous theories; for they begin with arbitrary interferences on the part of the banks. This is, perhaps, one of the main reasons for the prevailing scepti-

---

* *Der gegenwärtige Stand der Konjunkturforschung in Deutschland*, *op. cit.* p. 349.

cism concerning the value of such theories. A theory which has to call upon the *deus ex machina*[*] of a false step by bankers, in order to reach its conclusions is, perhaps, inevitably suspect. Yet Professor Mises himself — who is certainly to be regarded as the most respected and consistent exponent of the monetary theory of the Trade Cycle in Germany — has, in his latest work, afforded ample justification for this view of his theory by attributing the periodic recurrence of the Trade Cycle to the general tendency of Central Banks to depress the money rate of interest below the natural rate.[†] Both the protagonists and the opponents of the Monetary Theory of the Trade Cycle thus agree in regarding these explanations as falling ultimately within the exogenous and not the endogenous group. The fact that this is not an inherent necessity of the monetary starting-point is however shown by the

[*] Cf. Neisser, *Der Tauschwert des Geldes*, Jena, 1928, p. 161.

[†] While it seems to me that in the analysis of the effects of a money rate of interest diverging from the natural rate Professor Mises has made considerable progress as compared with the position adopted by Wicksell, the latter succeeded better than Mises did in explaining the origin of this divergence. We shall go into Wicksell's explanation in somewhat more detail below.

undoubtedly endogenous nature of the various older Trade Cycle theories, such as that of Wicksell. But since this suffers from other deficiencies, which have already been indicated, the question whether the exogenous character of modern theories is, or is not, an inherent necessity of their nature remains an open one.* It seems to me that this classification of monetary Trade Cycle theory depends exclusively on the fact that a single, specially striking, case is treated as the normal; while, in fact, it is quite unnecessary to adduce interference on the part of the banks in order to bring about a situation of alternating boom and crisis. By disregarding those divergencies between the natural and money rate of interest which arise automatically in the course of economic development, and by emphasizing those caused by an artificial lowering of the money rate, the Monetary Theory of the Trade Cycle deprives itself of one of its strongest arguments; namely, the fact that the process which it describes *must*

---

* Part of the two following paragraphs repeats word for word my contribution to the discussion on 'Credit and the Trade Cycle' at the Zürich Assembly of the 'Verein für Sozialpolitik,' (cf. *Schriften des Vereins für Sozialpolitik*, vol. 175, p. 370–71).

always recur under the existing credit organization, and that it thus represents a tendency inherent in the economic system, and is in the fullest sense of the word an *endogenous* theory.

✗ It is an apparently unimportant difference in exposition which leads one to this view that the Monetary Theory can lay claim to an endogenous position. The situation in which the money rate of interest is below the natural rate need not, by any means, originate in a *deliberate lowering* of the rate of interest by the banks. The same effect can be obviously produced by an improvement in the expectations of profit or by a diminution in the rate of saving, which may drive the 'natural rate' (at which the demand for and the supply of savings are equal) above its previous level; while the banks refrain from raising their rate of interest to a proportionate extent, but continue to lend at the previous rate, and thus enable a greater demand for loans to be satisfied than would be possible by the exclusive use of the available supply of savings. The decisive significance of the case quoted is not, in my view, due to the fact that it is probably the commonest in practice, but to the fact that it *must inevitably recur* under the existing credit organization.

I I I

The notion that the increase in circulation is due to arbitrary interference by the banks owes its origin to the widespread view that Banks of Issue are the exclusive or predominant agencies which can change the volume of the circulation; and that they do so of their own free will. But the Central Banks are by no means the only factor capable of bringing about a change in the volume of circulating media*; they are, in their turn, largely dependent upon other factors, although they can influence or compensate for these to a great extent. Altogether, there are three elements which regulate the volume of circulating media within a country — changes in the volume of cash, caused by

---

* This fact has already been pointed out by the representatives of the Banking School, and later by C. Juglar (*Du change et de la liberté d'émission*, Paris, 1868. Chap. III, *passim;* and *Des crises commerciales et leur retour périodique*, 2nd edit. Paris, 1889, p. 57). Wicksell (*Geldzins und Güterpreise*, p. 101) also points, first of all, to the deposit business of the banks as the cause of the 'elasticity' of the volume of currency media.

inflows and outflows of gold; changes in the note circulation of the Central Banks: and last, and in many ways most important, the often-disputed 'creation' of deposits by other banks. The inter-relations of these are, naturally, complicated.

As regards original changes in the first two factors — that is, changes which are not set in motion by changes in one of the other factors — there is comparatively little to say. It has already been pointed out that, in principle, an increase in the volume of cash, occasioned by an increase in the volume of trade, also implies a lowering of the money rate of interest — which gives rise to shifts in the structure of production which seem, though only temporarily, to be advantageous. It must certainly appear very problematical whether the deviations in the money rate of interest thus occasioned would, as a rule, be large enough to cause fluctuations of an empirically ascertainable magnitude. Central Banks, on the other hand, are by law or custom bound to preserve such a close connection between note issues and cash holdings that we have no reason to assume that they, and they alone, provide the original impetus. Of course, it is possible to assume, with Professor Mises, that the Central Banks, under the pressure of an inflationist ideology, are always trying to expand credit and thus provide the impetus for a new upward swing of the Trade Cycle; and this assumption may be correct in many cases. The credit expansion is then conditioned by special circumstances, which need not always be present; and the cyclical fluctuations caused by it are, therefore, not the necessary consequence of an inherent tendency of our credit system, for the removal of the special circumstances would eliminate them. But before deciding in favour of this special assumption — which requires a proof of its own, to be given separately in the case of each cycle — we have to ask whether, in some other part of our credit system, such extensions may not take place automatically under certain conditions — without the necessity for any special assumption of the inadequate functioning of any part of the system. To me this certainly appears to be true as regards the third factor of money expansion — the 'credit creation' of the commercial banks.

There are few questions upon which scientific

literature, especially in Germany, is so lacking in clarity as on the possibility and importance of an increase in circulating media due to the granting of additional credits by the banks of deposit. To give an answer to the question whether credit-creation is a regular consequence of the existing organization of banking, we shall have to attempt to clear up our conception of the methods and extent of such credit creation by deposit banks. Besides dealing with the fundamental question of the possibility of credit creation and the limits to which it can extend, we shall have to discuss two special questions which are important for our further investigations: namely, whether the practical importance of credit creation depends upon certain practices of banking technique, as is often assumed; and secondly, whether it is, in fact, possible to determine whether a given issue of credit represents credit freshly created or not.

If in the course of our investigation, it is possible to prove that the rate of interest charged by the banks to their borrowers is not promptly adjusted to all changes in the economic data (as it would be if the volume of money in circulation were constant)

— either because the supply of bank credits is, within certain limits, fundamentally independent of changes in the supply of savings, or because the banks have no particular interest in keeping the supply of bank credit in equilibrium with the supply of savings and because it is, in any case, impossible for them to do so — then we shall have proved that, under the existing credit organization, monetary fluctuations must inevitably occur and must represent an immanent feature of our economic system — a feature deserving of the closest examination.

I V

The main reason for the existing confusion with regard to the creation of deposits is to be found in the lack of any distinction between the possibilities open to a single bank and those open to the banking system as a whole.* This is

---

* As it is impossible to deal exhaustively with this problem, it must be sufficient to draw attention to the main literature of the subject. The first author known to me who definitely stated that 'the balances in the bank are to be considered in very much the same light with the paper circulation,' was Henry Thornton (see his evidence before the Committee on the Bank Restriction, 1797). The development of a more definite theory of credit creation by the banks began, however,

CAUSE OF CYCLICAL FLUCTUATIONS

connected with the fact that, in Germany, the
whole theory has been taken over bodily from
England, where, owing to differences in banking

with the criticisms levelled by the Banking School against the Currency
School, and represent the former's only correct contribution to the
science of economics. As Professor T. E. Gregory has recently shown
(*Introduction to Tooke and Newmarch's History of Prices*, London, 1928,
pp. 11 *et seq.*) it was James Pennington who originally developed this
thesis, first in an appendix to T. Tooke's *Letter to Lord Grenville
on the Effects ascribed to the Resumption of Cash Payments*, then in
further contributions to R. Torrens' *Letter to the Rt. Hon. Viscount
Melbourne* (London, 1837) and finally in an appendix to the third
volume of Tooke's *History of Prices* (1838). If one wanted to trace
the further progress of this theory during the nineteenth century,
one would have to draw particular attention to the writings of H. D.
Macleod (cf., in particular, his *Dictionary of Political Economy*,
London 1863, article on *Credit*), C. F. Dunbar and F. Ferrara.

Modern developments follow the exposition of H. J. Davenport
(*The Economics of Enterprise*, New York, 1915, pp. 250 *et seq.*); and
mention should, in particular, be made of C. O. Phillips's *Bank Credit*,
New York, 1920 (especially Chap. 111, 'The Philosophy of Bank
Credit'), of W. F. Crick (*The Genesis of Bank Deposits*, 'Economica',
vol. vii, No. 20–June 1927) and R. G. Rodley (*The Banking Process*,
New York, 1928). Apart from these, we must include in our list the
well-known works of Hartley Withers, Irving Fisher and R. G. Hawtrey and, in German literature, K. Wicksell (*Geldzins und Güterpreise*,
p. 101), A. Weber (*Depositenbanken und Spekulationsbanken*, 2nd edit.,
1922), the works which we have already mentioned of Mises and Hahn,
G. Haberler's essay on the latter (*Hahns Volkswirtschaftliche Theorie
des Bankkredits*, Archiv für Sozialwissenschaften, vol. 57, 1927) and,
finally, H. Neisser (*Der Tauschwert des Geldes*, Jena, 1928).

The theory has been severely criticized especially by Professor
Cannan, W. Leaf, and more recently by R. Reisch (*Die 'Deposit' –
legende in der Banktheorie*, Zeitschrift für Nationalökonomie, vol. i,
1930.)

technique, the limits imposed on any individual bank are, perhaps, somewhat less narrow, so that the general possibilities open to the banking system as a whole have not been indicated with the degree of emphasis which their importance deserves. In Germany, following the popular exposition of Mr. Hartley Withers, the most generally accepted view starts from English banking practice which (except in the case of 'overdrafts') credits the account of the customer with the amount borrowed before the latter is actually utilized. Granted this assumption, the process leading to an increase of circulating media is comparatively easy to survey and therefore hardly ever disputed. So long and in so far as the credits which a bank is able to grant, considering its cash position, remain on current account — and in the United States, for example, it is a regular condition for the granting of a loan that the current account of the borrower shall never fall below a certain relatively high percentage of the sum borrowed* — every new grant of credit must, of course, bring about an equivalent increase of deposits and a propor-

* Cf. C. O. Phillips, *op. cit.*, p. 50.

tionately smaller diminution of cash reserves. Against these 'deduced deposits' (Phillips) which regularly occur in the normal course of business, the banks naturally have to keep only a certain percentage of cash reserve; and thus it is clear that every bank can, on the basis of a given increase of deposits resulting from public payments, grant new credits to an amount exceeding this increase in deposits.

Against this method of proof it can rightly be objected that, while banking practices of this kind may well lead to the possibility of credit creation, the conditions which this argument assumes are not present on the Continent. It has been justifiably and repeatedly emphasized that there is no reason why the borrower, so long as he is not forced to do so, should borrow money at a higher rate of interest merely to leave that money on deposit at a lower rate.†

If the possibility of creating credit depended

† R. Reisch in 'Die Wirtschaftliche Bedeutung des Kredites im Lichte von Theorie und Praxis' (*Mitteilungen des Verbandes österreichischen Banken und Bankiers*, 10th year, Nos. 2–3, Vienna, 1928, p. 38) and A. Jöhr in his verbal report on Credit and the Cycle, in the Zürich Assembly of the Verein für Sozialpolitik (Schriften, vol. 175, p. 311).

only on the fact that borrowers leave part of their loans on current account for a time, then credit creation would be practically impossible on the Continent;* while even in England and the United States it would have only a very secondary importance. It should be noted that this applies to the case in which the borrower pays the sum borrowed into another account in the *same* bank, so that it is transferred from one to the other without diminishing the total volume of deposits in the bank concerned. We need not, therefore, go separately into this case.

But, in adopting this line of argument, by far the most important process by which deposits are created in the course of current banking business even in Anglo-Saxon countries is neglected, and the sole way in which they are created on the Continent is left entirely out of consideration. The latter could easily be overlooked, since the ability of individual banks to make an increase in their deposits the basis of a far greater amount

* As Bouniatian, evidently for this reason, actually assumes, (cf. his essay, 'Industrielle Schwankungen, Bankkredit und Warenpreise', Archiv für Sozialwissenschaften und Sozialpolitik, vol. 58, Tübingen, 1927, p. 463.)

of new credit can only be accounted for by means of the assumptions used above, while in the banking system as a whole the same process occurs independently. In the following pages, therefore, we shall examine how an increase in deposits, paid in in cash, influences the lending capacity of the whole banking system; starting from the assumption, more appropriate to Continental conditions, that the sums granted will be credited to the account of the borrower only at the time when, and to the extent that, he makes use of them.

V

We may start as before by examining the procedure of a single bank. At this bank a certain amount of cash is newly deposited; a sum, let us say, equal to 5 per cent of its previous total deposits. If the policy of the bank was to keep a reserve of 10 per cent against deposits, that ratio has now been increased, by the new deposit, to 14.3 per cent, and the bank is therefore in a position, in accordance with its policy, to grant new credits. If we assume further that it re-lends 90 per cent of the newly deposited money and that the whole of this is immediately utilized by the borrower (in order, let us say, to increase his purchases of raw materials) then the ratio of cash to deposits has again sunk to 10 per cent. In so far as the bank does not change its policy its individual lending capacity is exhausted, in these circumstances, before it has even re-lent the whole of the amount newly deposited.

The effect of the sums newly deposited at one bank on the lending capacity of the whole banking system is, however, not exhausted by this transaction. If the borrower does not use the credit in a way which leads quickly to the market for consumers' goods, such as wage payments, but devotes it instead to the purchase of raw materials or half-finished products, then it is to be assumed that payment will be made by cheque and that the seller will hand over the sum received to his own bank for encashment, the amount being credited to his own account. The next consequence must be that the clearing-house position of this bank improves by exactly the amount transferred, and it therefore obtains an equivalent amount of cash from the bank which originally granted the credit.

For the second bank, therefore, the sum originating in the granting of credit and paid into its accounts (representing, as we remember, 90 per cent of the original deposit) is just as much an original deposit, based on cash payments, as it was to the bank which we originally considered. It will, therefore, be regarded as a basis for additional lending and used in just the same way as any other new deposit. If the second bank also keeps 10 per cent of its deposits as cash reserves, it too will be in a position to lend 90 per cent of the new deposit, and the same process will be continued as long as the amounts are merely transferred from bank to bank and are not taken out in cash. As every bank re-lends 90 per cent of the amount paid into it and thus causes an equivalent increase in deposits for some other bank, the original deposit will give rise to credits representing $0.9+0.9^2+0.9^3+0.9^4$ . . . . . times the original amount. As the sum of this converging infinite series is 9, the banks will be enabled, in an extreme case, to create, against an amount of cash flowing in from an outside source, credits equal to nine times that amount. This becomes clear when we consider that the process can only stop when the last part of this cash is required for the 10 per cent reserve of the deposits.

For simplicity's sake we have made use of an assumption which is undoubtedly incorrect, but which affects our conclusion only in so far as it reduces the actual amount of new credit which the banks can create with a reserve ratio of 10 per cent. Its omission leaves our fundamental conclusion intact; i.e. that they can grant credit to an amount several times greater than the sum originally deposited. In fact some part of the credit at least, if not on the first then on subsequent occasions, will always be withdrawn in cash and not deposited with other banks. For example, if 70 per cent is always redeposited instead of the full 90 per cent this amount being re-lent by every bank and the remainder being used in cash transactions, then the increase in deposits will give rise to additional credits equal to only $0.7 + 0.7^2 + 0.7^3 \ldots \ldots$ times (i.e. two and one-third times) the original. So long as any part of the credits granted are not withdrawn in cash but redeposited with the banks, the latter will be able to create additional credits, of a larger or smaller amount, as a consequence of every increase in their cash holdings.* The lifetime of this pyramid of credit is limited to that of the first credit granted, save in the case (which can be assumed as long as there are no withdrawals from deposits) where it is immediately replaced by a fresh credit. If, however, deposits unexpectedly diminish at any part of the banking system, the process will be reversed, and the original diminution of deposits will occasion a contraction of credit correspondingly exceeding the amount withdrawn.†

* The maximum amount of credit, to the creation of which the increase in the cash holdings of the banks may give rise under such an assumption, is easily found by inserting the factor representing the proportion of the original deposit which is re-lent and redeposited with another bank into the mathematical formula expressing the limit which a convergent geometrical series approaches, viz., $\frac{1}{x-1}$ The result gives the total of credits which originate in the series of transactions, including the original deposit and, in order to arrive at the amount of additional credits, 1 has to be subtracted from the result. It is thus easily seen that even if, for example, only 1-9th of the 90 per cent re-lent by the first bank, or 10 per cent of the original deposit, is redeposited with another bank – and this process is repeated, *additional* credits amounting to 0.111 times the original deposit will be created.

† On this question, and on the interesting effects of a transference of deposits from one bank to another, cf. the more elaborate treatment of C. O. Phillips, *op. cit*, p. 64 *seq.*; also the remarks of W. F. Crick, *loc. cit*, p. 196.

In this connection we must note for further emphasis later the fact that the proportion in which the credits granted are transferred to other accounts — and not paid out in cash — must be regarded as subject to very wide fluctuations as between different individuals at a given moment, as well as between various periods of time for the economic system as a whole. We return later to the significance of this fact.

What has been said above should be sufficient to show that the possibility of creating credits over and above the sums deposited — which, under Continental banking conditions, is not open to any individual bank — is, however, open to the whole banking system of the country to a considerable extent. The fact that a single bank cannot do what is automatically done by the banking system as a whole also explains another circumstance, which might otherwise easily be cited as a proof of the impossibility of additional credit creation. If every bank could re-lend several times the amount deposited, there would be no reason against its offering a much higher rate of interest on deposits than it actually does, or, in particular, under the existing discount rates of the Central Banks, against its procuring cash in unlimited quantities by way of re-discount; for it would only have to charge its customers a small part of the rate of interest charged by the banks in order to make the business pay. This apparent contradiction between theory and practice is cleared up as soon as one realizes that an increase of deposits by a single bank only offers possibilities for credit creation to the banking system as a whole. But the importance of this circumstance transcends the mere clearing up of this difficulty.

V I

As credits created on the basis of additional deposits do not normally appear in the accounts of the same bank which granted the credit, it is fundamentally impossible to distinguish, in individual cases, between 'those deposits which arose through cash payment and those which find their origin in credit.'* But this consideration

* Neisser (*op. cit.*, p. 53) deserves credit for clearing up an untenable conception, which was quite recently held by no less an authority than Professor J. Schumpeter (*Theorie der wirtschaftlicaen Entwicklung*, Münich and Leipzig, 2nd edit., 1926, p. 144).

rules out, *a priori*, the possibility of bankers limiting the amount of credit granted by them to the amount of 'real' accumulated deposits — that is, those arising from the accommodation of temporarily unused money. The same fact enables us to understand why it is generally just those economic writers who are also practical bankers who are most unwilling to admit in any circumstances that they are in a position to create credits.* 'The banker simply does not notice that through this process there is an increase in the amount of money in circulation.'† Once the impetus has been given to any part of the banking system, mere adherence to the routine of banking technique will lead to the creation of additional deposits

* Cf., for example, Walter Leaf, the late chairman of the Westminster Bank, in his book *Banking* (Home University Library, London, 1926), or the contributions of A. Jöhr and B. Dernburg to the Zurich Debate on the Trade Cycle. (*Schriften des Vereines für Sozialpolitik*, vol. 175, 1929, pp. 311 and 329). These arguments were perfectly correctly answered by another 'practical' banker, K. Schlesinger (ibid., p. 355). Professor A. Hahn, on the other hand, falls into the opposite error. The standpoint of Professor R. Reisch will be discussed later.

† Neisser, *op. cit.*, p. 54. He goes on to say, quite correctly, that 'the mere fact that cheque-deposits represent money, without being covered by cash up to 100 per cent, already explains the money-creating nature of bank credit.'

without the possibility arising, at any point, of determining whether any particular credit should properly be regarded as 'additional.' Every time money which has been deposited is re-lent — provided that the depositor is not prevented from using his deposits for making payments — this process is to be regarded as the creation of additional purchasing power; and it is merely this comparatively simple operation which is at the root of the banks' ability to create purchasing power — although the process appears so mysterious to many people. It is thus by no means necessary that the banks should grant these credits, as Dr. Dernburg seems to assume, in an 'improper or wanton' way.

It is of course quite another question whether bankers can, or do, create additional credits of their own free will. The objections to this theory of additional credits, which are levelled against the statement that the banks create credit 'as they please', although holding good at a given rate of interest, do not in the least affect that part of the theory which we need for our analysis. If Professor Reisch, for example, emphasizes that bank deposits generally increase only 'according to the needs of business,'* or if Prof. Bouniatian objects that 'it does not depend on the banks, but on the demands made by commerce and industry, how far banks expand credit,'† then these assertions, coming as they do from opponents of the theory of bank credits, already contain all that is needed for a deductive proof of the necessity for the recurrence of credit cycles. What interests us is precisely the question whether the banks are able to satisfy the increased demands of business men for credits without being obliged immediately to raise their interest charges — as would be the case if the supply of savings and the demand for credits were to be in direct contact, without the agency of the banks (as for example in the hypothetical 'savings market' of theory); or whether it is even possible for the banks to raise their interest charges immediately the demand for credits increases. Even the bitterest opponents of this theory of bank credit are forced to admit that 'there can be no doubt that, with the upward

* *Op. cit.*, p. 39.   † *Op. cit.*, p. 465.

swing of the Trade Cycle, a certain expansion of bank credits takes place.'*

We must not, however, be satisfied with registering the general agreement of opinion on this point. Before passing on to analyse the consequences of this phenomenon we must ask whether the causes which bring it about that banks increase their deposits through additional credits in periods of boom and thus postpone, at any rate temporarily, the rise in the rate of interest which would otherwise necessarily take place, are inherent in the nature of the system, or not.

VII

So far, the starting point of our argument concerning the origin of additional credits has been the assumption that the banks receive an increased in-flow of cash which they then use as a basis for new credits on a much larger scale. We must now inquire how banks behave when an increased demand for credit makes itself felt.

* Dernburg, *op. cit.*, p. 329. He merely adds to this statement the remark that the banks and the Central Bank should see to it that this expansion is 'kept in order'!

Assuming, as is preferable, that this increased demand was not caused by a lowering of their own interest rates, this additional demand is always a sign that the natural rate of interest has risen — that is, that a given amount of money can now find more profitable employment than hitherto. The reasons for this can be of very different kinds.* New inventions or discoveries, the opening up of new markets, or even bad harvests,† the appearance of entrepreneurs of genius who originate 'new combinations' (Schumpeter), a fall in wage rates due to heavy immigration; and the destruction of great blocks of capital by a natural catastrophe, or many others. We have already seen that none of these reasons is in itself sufficient to account for an *excessive* increase of investing activity, which necessarily engenders a subsequent crisis; but that they can lead to this result only through the increase in the means of credit which they inaugurate.

* 'A great variety of causes,' observes R. G. Hawtrey, very correctly (*Trade and Credit*, London, 1928, p. 175).

† Regarding the influence of harvests on the Trade Cycle, cf. the useful compilation of various contradictory theories by V. P. Timoshenko, *The Role of Agricultural Fluctuations in The Business Cycle* (Michigan Business Studies, vol. ii, No. 9, 1930).

But how is it possible for the banks to extend credit, as they undoubtedly do, following an increase in demand, when no additional cash is flowing into their vaults? There is no reason to assume that the same cause which has led to an increased demand for credit will also influence another factor, the cash position of the banks — which as we know is the only factor determining the extent to which credit can be granted.* So long as the banks maintain a constant proportion between their cash reserves and their deposits it would be impossible to satisfy the new demand for credit. The fact that in reality deposits always do expand relatively to cash reserves, in the course of the boom, so that the liquidity of the banks is always impaired in such periods, does not of course constitute a sufficient starting point for an argument in which the increase in credits is

* It is of course possible that an improvement in the conditions of production and profit-making will also indirectly cause an increased flow of cash to the banks, for a flow of funds for investment, as well as an increased flow of payments for goods, can be expected from abroad. But, in the first place, this increased flow of cash can only be expected in a comparatively late stage of the boom, so that it can hardly explain the latter's origin; and in the second place, such an explanation could only be adduced in the case of a single country, and not for the world economy as a whole, or in a closed system.

regarded as *the* decisive factor determining the course and extent of the cyclical movement. We must attempt to understand fully the causes and nature of this credit expansion and in particular, its limits.

The key to this problem can only be found in the fact that the ratio of reserves to deposits does not represent a constant magnitude, but, as experience shows, is itself variable. But we shall achieve a satisfactory solution only by showing that the reason for this variability in the reserve is not based on the arbitrary decisions of the bankers, but is itself conditioned by the general economic situation. Such an examination of the causes determining the size of the reserve ratio desired by the banks is all the more important since we had no theoretical warrant for our previous assumption that it always tends to be constant.

It is best to begin our investigation by considering once again the situation of a single bank, and asking how the manager will react when the credit requirements of the customers increase in consequence of an all-round improvement in the business situation.* For reasons which will shortly become clear, we must assume that the bank under consideration is the first to feel the new credit-requirements of industry, because, let us say, its customers are drawn from just those industries which first feel the effects of the new recovery. Among the factors which determine the volume of loans granted by the bank, only one has changed; whereas previously, at the same rate of interest and with the same security, no new borrowers came forward, now, under the same conditions of borrowing, more loans can be placed. On the other hand, the cash holdings of the bank remain unchanged. This does not mean, however, that the considerations of liquidity which dictate the amount of loans to be granted will lead to the same result now as when fresh loans could only have been placed at a lower rate of interest or with inferior security than was the case with loans already granted. In this connection, finally, we must mention that the sums which we have, for

* The problems with which the manager of a single bank is confronted in deciding the bank's credit policy are very neatly analysed by Mr. W. F. Crick, *op. cit.*, p. 197, *et seq*

simplicity's sake, hitherto called cash balances, and which form the bank's liquid reserve, are by no means exclusively composed of cash — and are not even of a constant magnitude, unrelated to the size of the profits which they make possible. The danger that, in case of need, the reserves may have to be replenished by rediscounting bills through the Central Bank*; or that, in order to correct an unfavourable clearing-house balance, day-money may have to be borrowed at a given rate of interest, is far less abhorrent when it is possible to extend credits at an undiminished rate of interest than when such an extension would involve a lowering of that rate. But even disregarding this possibility and assuming that the bank recognizes that it can satisfy its eventual need for cash only at correspondingly higher rates, we can see that the greater loss of profit entailed by keeping the cash reserve intact will, as a rule, lead the

* On this point see J. S. Lawrence, 'Borrowed Reserves and Bank Expansion' (*Quarterly Journal of Economics*, vol. xlii, Cambridge, Mass., 1928) where Mr. Phillips's exposition, mentioned above, is extensively criticized; also the rejoinder of Mr. F. A. Bradford, published under the same title in the next volume (xliii) of the same journal.

bank to a policy which involves diminishing the size of this non-earning asset. Besides this, we have the consideration that, in the upward phase of the cycle, the risks of borrowing are less; and therefore a smaller cash reserve may suffice to provide the same degree of security. But it is above all for reasons of competition that the bank which first feels the effect of an increased demand for credits cannot afford to reply by putting up its interest charges; for it would risk losing its best customers to other banks which had not yet experienced a similarly increased demand for credits. There can be little doubt, therefore, that the bank or banks which are the first to feel the effects of new credit requirements will be forced to satisfy these even at the cost of reducing their liquidity.

VIII

But once one bank or group of banks has started the expansion, then all the other banks receive, as already described, a flow of cash which at first enables them to expand credit on their own account without impairing their liquidity. They make use of this possibility the more readily since they, in turn, soon feel the increased demand for credit. Once the process of expansion has become general, however, the banks soon realize that, for the moment at any rate, they can safely modify their ideas of liquidity. While expansion by a single bank will soon confront it with a clearing-house deficit of practically the same magnitude as the original new credit, a general expansion carried on at about the same rate by all banks will give rise to clearing-house claims which, although larger, mainly compensate one another and so induce only a relatively unimportant cash drain. If a bank does not at first keep pace with the expansion it will, sooner or later, be induced to do so, since it will continue to receive cash at the clearing house as long as it does not adjust itself to the new standard of liquidity.

So long as this process goes on, it is practically impossible for any single bank, acting alone, to apply the only control by which the demand for credit can, in the long run, be successfully kept within bounds; that is, an increase in its interest charges. Concerted action in this direction, which for competitive reasons is the only action possible, will ensue only when the increased cash requirements of business compel the banks to protect their cash balances by checking further credit expansion, or when the Central Bank has preceded them by raising its discount rate. This, again, will only happen, as a rule, when the banks have been induced by the growing drain on their cash to increase their re-discount. Experience shows, moreover, that the relation between cheque-payments and cash payments alters in favour of the latter as the boom proceeds, so that an increased proportion of the cash is finally withdrawn from the banks.*

This phenomenon is easily explained in theory by the fact that a low rate of interest first raises the prices of capital goods and only subsequently those of consumption goods, so that the first

* Cf. the statements contained in the well-known 10th yearly Report of the Federal Reserve Board, for 1923 (Washington, 1924) p. 25: 'This is the usual sequence – an increase in deposits followed by an increase in currency. Ordinarily the first effect of an increase in business activity on the banking position is a growth in loans and deposits . . . Then comes a time when the increase in business activity and the fuller employment of labour and increased pay-roll call for an increase in actual pocket money to support the increased wage disbursements and the increased volume of purchases in detail.'

175

increases occur in the kind of payments which are effected in large blocks.* It may lead to the consequence that banks are not only prevented from granting new credits, but even forced to diminish credits already granted. This fact may well aggravate the crisis; but it is by no means necessary in order to bring it about. For this *it is quite enough that the banks should cease to extend the volume of credit;* and sooner or later this must happen. Only so long as the volume of circulating media is increasing can the money rate of interest be kept below the equilibrium rate; once it has ceased to increase, the money rate must, despite the increased total volume in circulation, rise again to its natural level and thus render unprofitable (temporarily, at least) those investments which were created with the aid of additional credit.†

---

* Neisser (*op. cit.*, p. 162) doubts this, but his criticism results from an inadequate grasp of the effects of an unduly low money rate of interest. But even if he were right on this point, the arguments of monetary Trade Cycle theory would remain unaffected, since the latter, as is shown in the text, does not depend on this assumption for its proof.

† We need not stay to examine the case of a continuous increase in circulating media, which can only occur under a free paper standard.

I X

The assertion which forms the starting point of the 'Additional Credit Theory of the Trade Cycle', and whose proof has been attempted in the preceding pages, has never in fact been seriously questioned; but hardly any attempts have been made to follow up all the unpleasant consequences of the state of affairs it indicates. Yet what is implied when the beneficial effects of bank credits are praised but that thanks to the activities of banks an increased demand for credit is followed by a greater increase in its supply than would be warranted by the supply of contemporary saving? Wherein lie the often praised effects of credit, if not in the fact that it provides means for enterprises for which no provision could be found if the choices of the different economic subjects were strictly followed? By creating additional credits in response to an increased demand, and thus opening up new possibilities of improving and extending production, the banks ensure that impulses towards expansion of the productive apparatus shall not be so immediately and insuperably balked by a rise of interest rates as they would be if progress were limited by the slow increase in the flow of savings. But this same policy stultifies the automatic mechanism of adjustment which keeps the various parts of the system in equilibrium, and makes possible disproportionate developments which must, sooner or later, bring about a reaction.

Elasticity in the credit supply of an economic system, is not only universally demanded but also — as the result of an organization of the credit system which has adapted itself to this requirement — an undeniable fact, whose necessity or advantages are not discussed here.* But we must be quite clear on one point. *An economic system with an elastic currency must, in many instances, react to external influences quite differently from an economy in which economic forces impinge on goods in their full force — without any intermediary; and we must, a priori, expect any process started by an*

* Cf. K. Wicksell, *Geldzins und Güterpreise*, p. 101, 'The more elastic is the currency system the longer can a more or less constant difference persist between the two interest rates and the greater, therefore, will be the influence of this discrepancy on prices.'

outside impulse to run an entirely different course in such an economy from that described by a theory which only takes into account changes originating on the side of goods. Once, owing to the disturbing influence of money, even a single price has been fixed at a different level from that which it would have formed in a barter economy, a shift in the whole structure of production is inevitable; and this shift, so long as we make use of static theory and the methods proper to it, can only be explained as an exclusive consequence of the peculiar influence of money. The immediate consequence of an adjustment of the volume of money to the 'requirements' of industry is the failure of the 'interest brake' to operate as promptly as it would in an economy operating without credit. This means, however, that new adjustments are undertaken on a larger scale than can be completed; a boom is thus made possible, with the inevitably recurring 'crisis.' *The determining cause of the cyclical fluctuation is, therefore, the fact that on account of the elasticity of the volume of currency media the rate of interest demanded by the banks is not necessarily always equal to the* *equilibrium rate, but is, in the short run, determined by considerations of banking liquidity.* *

 * In a previous work (*Die Währungspolitik der Vereinigten Staaten, op. cit.*, p. 260), I have already dealt with the elasticity of bank credit as *the* cause of cyclical fluctuations. This view of its determining importance is now also put forward by Professor F. A. Fetter in a very interesting essay, 'Interest Theories and Price Movements' (*American Economic Review*, vol. xvii, supplement, March 1927; see especially, pp. 95 *et seq.*). Prof. Fetter, of course, is also under the influence of the prevailing dogma which holds that the existence of a stable price level is sufficient proof of the absence of all monetary influences. The crucial part of his argument, not having received the attention which it deserves in recent monetary literature, is reprinted here:

'The foregoing presents the extreme case of the expansion and contraction of bank loans in relation to prices, *but in principle quite small changes in the loan policies of banks affecting the volume of commercial loans*, discount rates, and percentages of reserves, *are of the same nature*. They cause and constitute inflation and deflation of the exchange medium and of commercial purchasing power, not originating in the amount of standard money but in the elasticity of banking loan funds. *This word "elasticity" has long been used in discussions of banking policy to designate a quality assumed to be wholly desirable in bank note issues and customers' credits*, but with only vague suggestions as to what is the need, standard, or means, with reference to which bank loans should expand and contract.

'Rather, it may be more exact to say, the tacit assumption has been that the bank loan funds should be elastic in response to the "needs of business.' *But "the needs of business" appears to be nothing but another name for changes in customers' eagerness for loans;* and this eagerness increases when prices are beginning, or are expected, to rise and often continues to gather momentum while prices rise and until, because of vanishing reserve percentages (and other factors), the limit of this elasticity and also the limit of price increase are in sight. In this situation the most conservative business operations become intermixed with elements of investment speculation, motivated by the

The main question set by this inquiry is thus answered. A deductive explanation embracing all the phenomena of the Trade Cycle would require far-reaching logical investigations entirely transcending the scope of this work, which aims merely at an exposition of the monetary basis of Trade Cycle theory. For the present, we must content ourselves with a reference to existing literature on the subject.* In the present work

rise of prices and the hope of profit that will be made possible by a further rise. *Throughout this process the much-esteemed elasticity of bank funds is the very condition causing, or making possible, the rising prices which stimulate the so-called "needs of business". Truly a vicious circle, to be broken only by crisis and collapse when bank loans reach a limit and prices fall.'* (My italics.)

Further, we should point out the connection between our theory and a famous thesis of Mr. R. G. Hawtrey. The phrase 'so long as credit is regulated with reference to reserve proportions, the trade cycle is bound to recur' (*Monetary Reconstruction*, 2nd edit., London, 1926, p. 135) is undoubtedly correct, though perhaps in a sense somewhat different from that intended by the author; for a regulation of this volume of loans exclusively from the point of view of liquidity can never effect a prompt adjustment of the rates charged on loans to the changes in the equilibrium rate, and thus cannot help providing opportunities for the temporary creation of additional credits as soon as (at a given rate of interest) the demand for credit surpasses the accumulation of savings; that is, when the natural rate of interest has risen. See, finally, the remarks of Professor W. Röpke, *Kredit und Konjunktur*, *op. cit.*, p. 274.

* Besides Professor Mises' *Theorie des Geldes und der Umlaufsmittel* we must mention the last chapter of S. Budge's *Gründzuge der Theoretischen Nationalökonomie* (Jena, 1925) and Prof. Strigl's

we shall only draw a few conclusions which follow from our previous arguments, some with regard to practical policy, some with regard to further scientific research. Before going on to this, however, we shall venture a few remarks on the question whether the result of our investigations unequivocally settles the controversy between the protagonists and opponents of the monetary Trade Cycle theory in favour of the former.

X

It must be emphasized first and foremost that there is no necessary reason why the initiating change, the original disturbance eliciting a cyclical fluctuation in a stationary economy, should be of monetary origin. Nor, in practice, is this even generally the case. The initial change need have no specific character at all, it may be any one among a thousand different factors which may at

paper on "Die Produktion unter dem Einfluss einer Kredit-expansion' in vol. 173-ii of the *Schriften des Vereins für Sozial-politik*, concerning Trade Cycle theory and business research (Münich and Leipzig, 1928), a volume which has been repeatedly quoted above. Since the above was written, I have tried to carry the analysis of these phenomena a step further in *Prices and Production* (London, 1931).

any time increase the profitability of any group of enterprises. For it is not the occurrence of a 'change of data' which is significant, but the fact that the economic system, instead of reacting to this change with an immediate 'adjustment' (Schumpeter) — i.e. the formation of a new equilibrium — begins a particular movement of 'boom' which contains, within itself, the seeds of an inevitable reaction. This phenomenon, as we have seen, should undoubtedly be ascribed to monetary factors, and in particular to 'additional credits' which also necessarily determine the extent and duration of the cyclical fluctuation. Once this point is agreed upon, it naturally becomes quite irrelevant whether we label this explanation of the Trade Cycle as a monetary theory or not. What is important is to recognize that it is to monetary causes that we must ascribe the divergences of the pricing process, during the Trade Cycle, from the course deduced in static theory.

From the particular point of view from which we started, our theory must be regarded most decisively as a monetary one. As to the incorporation of Trade Cycle theory into the general framework of static equilibrium theory (for the clear formulation of which we are indebted to Professor A. Löwe, one of the strongest opponents of monetary Trade Cycle theory), we must maintain, in opposition to his view, not only that our own theory is undoubtedly a monetary one but that a theory other than monetary is hardly conceivable.* It must be conceded that the monetary theory as we have presented it — whether one prefers to call it a monetary theory or not, and whether or not one finds it a sufficient explanation of the empirically determined fluctuations — has this definite advantage: *it deals with problems which must, in any case, be dealt with for they are necessarily given when the central apparatus of economic analysis is applied to the explanation of the existing organization of exchange. Even if we had never noticed cyclical fluctuations, even if all the actual fluctuations of history were accepted as the consequences of natural events, a*

* Cf. my report: 'Uber den Einfluss monetärer Faktoren auf den Konjunkturzyklus' (*Schriften des Vereins für Sozialpolitik*, vol. 173-ii, p. 362 *et seq.*).

consequential analysis of the effects which follow from the peculiar workings of our existing credit organization would be bound to demonstrate that fluctuations caused by monetary factors are unavoidable.

It is, of course, an entirely different question whether these monetary fluctuations would, if not reinforced by other factors, attain the extent and duration which we observe in the historical cycles; or whether in the absence of these supplementary factors they would not be much weaker and less acute than they actually are. Perhaps the empirically observed strength of the cyclical fluctuations is really only due to periodic changes in external circumstances, such as short-period variations of climate, or changes in subjective data (as e.g., the sudden appearance of entrepreneurs of genius) or perhaps the interval between individual cyclical waves may be due to some natural law.* Whatever further hypothetical causes are adduced to explain the empirically observed course of the fluctuations, there can be no doubt

---

* From now to the end of the section the exposition follows, in part word for word, my contribution to the Zürich discussion of the 'Verein für Sozialpolitik.' (*op. cit.*, p. 372 *et seq.*)

(and this is the important and indispensable contribution of monetary Trade Cycle theory) that the modern economic system cannot be conceived without fluctuations ascribable to monetary influences; and therefore any other factors which may be found necessary to explain the empirically observed phenomena will have to be regarded as causes *additional* to the monetary cause. In other words, any non-monetary Trade Cycle theory must superimpose its system of explanation on that of the monetarily determined fluctuations; it cannot start simply from the static system as presented by pure equilibrium theory.

Once this is admitted, however, the question whether the monetary theory of the Trade Cycle is correct or not must, at any rate, be presented in a different form. For if the correctness of the inter-connections described by monetary theory is unquestioned, there still remains the problem whether it is also sufficient to explain all those phenomena which are observed empirically in the course of the Trade Cycle; it may perhaps need supplementing in order to make it an instrument suitable to explain the working of the modern economic system. It seems to me, however, that before we can successfully tackle this problem we ought to know exactly how much of the empirically observed fluctuations is due to the monetary factor, which is actually always at work; and therefore we shall have to work out in the fullest detail the theory of monetary fluctuations. It is hardly permissible, methodologically speaking, to go in search of other causes whose existence we may conjecture, before ascertaining exactly how far, and to what extent, the monetary factors are operative. It is our duty to work out in detail the necessary consequences of those causes of disturbance which we know, and to make this train of thought a definite part our logical system, before attempting to incorporate any other factors which may come into play.

XI

The fact, simple and indisputable as it is, that the 'elasticity' of the supply of currency media, resulting from the existing monetary organization, offers a sufficient reason for the genesis and recurrence of fluctuations in the whole economy is of the utmost importance — for it implies that no measure which can be conceived in practice would be able entirely to suppress these fluctuations.

It follows particularly from the point of view of the monetary theory of the Trade Cycle, that it is by no means justifiable to expect the total disappearance of cyclical fluctuations to accompany a stable price-level — a belief which Professor Löwe* seems to regard as the necessary consequence of the Monetary Theory of the Trade Cycle. Professor Röpke is undoubtedly right when he emphasizes the fact that 'even if a stable price level could be successfully imposed on the capitalist economy the causes making for cyclical fluctuations would not be removed.'† But to realize this, as the preceding argument shows, is by no means 'equivalent to a rejection of a 100 per cent monetary Trade Cycle theory.'‡ On the contrary, on this view, we must regard Professor Röpke's theory, which coincides in the

---

*'Uber den Einfluss monetärer Faktoren auf den Konjunkturzyklus.' *op. cit.*, p. 369.

Op. cit., p. 265.   ‡ Ibid., p. 278.

more important points with our own,* as itself constituting such a 100 per cent monetary Trade Cycle theory.

Once this is realized, we can also see how nonsensical it is to formulate the question of the causation of cyclical fluctuations in terms of 'guilt,' and to single out, e.g., the banks as those 'guilty' of causing fluctuations in economic development.† Nobody has ever asked them to pursue a policy other than that which, as we have seen, gives rise to cyclical fluctuations; and it is not within their power to do away with such fluctuations, seeing that the latter originate not from their policy but from the very nature of the modern organization of credit. So long as we make use of bank credit as a means of furthering economic development we shall have to put up with the resulting trade cycles. They are, in a sense, the price we pay for a speed of development exceeding that which people would voluntarily make possible through their savings, and which

---

* Cf. especially pp. 274 *et seq.* of the work mentioned.

† As Prof. S. Budge seems inclined to do (*op. cit.*, p. 216). His exposition in other respects largely coincides with ours.

therefore has to be extorted from them. And even if it is a mistake — as the recurrence of crises would demonstrate — to suppose that we can, in this way, overcome all obstacles standing in the way of progress, it is at least conceivable that the non-economic factors of progress, such as technical and commercial knowledge, are thereby benefited in a way which we should be reluctant to forgo.

If it were possible, as has been repeatedly asserted in recent English literature,* to keep the total amount of bank deposits entirely stable, that would constitute the only means of getting rid of cyclical fluctuations. This seems to us purely Utopian. It would necessitate the complete abolition of all bank-money — i.e. notes and cheques — and the reduction of the banks to the role of brokers, trading in savings. But even if we assume the fundamental possibility of this state of things, it remains very questionable whether many would wish to put it into effect if they were clear about its consequences. The stability of the economic system would be obtained

* Certain statements of Mr. R. G. Hawtrey seem to point to this, especially *op. cit.*, p. 121.

at the price of curbing economic progress. The rate of interest would be constantly above the level maintained under the existing system (for, generally speaking, even in times of depression some extension of credit takes place)*. The utilization of new inventions and the 'realization of new combinations' would be made more difficult, and thus there would disappear a psychological incentive towards progress, whose importance cannot be judged on purely economic grounds. It is no exaggeration to say that not only would it be impossible to put such a scheme into practice in the present state of economic enlightenment of the public, but even its theoretical justification would be doubtful.

As regards the practical bearing of our analysis on the Trade Cycle policy of the banks, all that can be deduced from it is that bankers will have to weigh carefully the relative advantages and disadvantages of granting credits on an increasing

---

* Cf. Professor A. C. Pigou *Industrial Fluctuations*, 2nd edit., p. 145: 'Banks do not in bad times reduce the amount of new real capital flowing to business men below what it would have been had there been no banks, but merely increase it to a smaller extent than they do in good times.'

scale, and to take into account the demand, now fairly widespread, for the early application of a check to credit expansion. But the utmost that can be achieved on these lines is only a mitigation, never the abolition, of the Trade Cycle. Apart from this, the only way of minimizing damage is through a far-reaching adjustment of the economic system to the recognized existence of cyclical movements; and for this purpose the most important condition is an increased insight into the nature of the Trade Cycle and a knowledge of its actual phase at any particular moment.*

* In this connection, apart from empirical research, the greatest consideration should be given to the plea made by O. Morgenstern (*op. cit.*, p. 123 *et seq.*) for giving increased publicity to company developments.

UNSETTLED PROBLEMS OF TRADE CYCLE THEORY

CHAPTER V

UNSETTLED PROBLEMS OF TRADE CYCLE THEORY

I

So much has already been said (in Ch. III, ¶ 4 and 6) about the most important of the outstanding problems of monetary influences on economic phenomena, that only a brief supplement is needed at this point. With regard to the problems of monetary theory in the narrower sense I may restrict myself chiefly to what has been said above, as I hope to publish the results of a separate investigation concerning this problem elsewhere.* A few remarks may, however, be ventured merely as a summing-up of what has already been said, and in doing this we shall touch on a number of other important

---

* Cf. *Das intertemporale Gleichgewichtssystem der Preise und die Bewegungen des Geldwertes*, Weltwirtschaftliches Archiv 1928; and more especially. *Prices and Production*, London, 1931, where I have attempted to develop some of the points touched upon in this chapter.

problems. The most significant result of our investigation must be the grasp of the elementary fact that *we have no right to assume that an economic system with an 'elastic' currency will ever exhibit those movements which can be immediately deduced from the propositions of static theory*. On the contrary, it is to be expected that movements will arise which would not be possible under the conditions usually assumed by that theory. It is particularly important to realize that this proposition is true whether the changes in the volume of money also effect changes in the so-called 'general value of money' or not. With the disappearance of the idea that money can only exert an active influence on economic movement when the value of money (as measured by one kind of price level) is changing, the theory that the general value of money is the sole object of explanation for monetary theory must fall to the ground. Its place must, henceforth, be taken by an analysis of *all* the effects of money on the course of economic development. All changes in the *volume* of effective monetary circulation, and only such changes, will therefore rank for consideration as changes in economic data capable of originating 'monetary influences'.

The next task of monetary theory is, therefore, a systematic investigation of the effects of changes in the volume of money. In the course of this approach, relationships will inevitably be contemplated which do not have the permanence of the equilibrium relationships. All these results, however (and this must be emphasized to prevent misunderstanding) will be reached by the aid of the methods of static analysis, for these are the only instruments available to economic theory. The only difference is that these methods will be applied to an entirely new set of circumstances which have never, up till now, received the attention they deserve. It is vitally necessary that such an investigation should keep clear of the notion that the adjustment of the supply of money to changes in 'money requirements' is an essential condition for the smooth working of the equilibrating process of the system, as presented in equilibrium theory.* It must always start from the

---

* This notion rests on a confusion between the demand for money and the demand for cash, i.e. that portion of the total amount of money

assumption that the natural determining factors will exert their full effect only when the effective volume of money remains unchanged, whatever may be the actual changes in the extent of economic activity.

Precise propositions as to the effects of changes in the volume of money can be laid down only when accurate information is available both as to the genesis of the change and the part of the economic system where it took place. For this reason little can be said about changes resulting from the decumulation of hoarded treasure or the discovery of new gold deposits. The way in which an individual will elect to spend money coming to him as a gift or as a result of other non-economic motives cannot be determined from deductive considerations. Similarly, little can be said *a priori* about bank credits granted to the State, so long as we have no information as to how they are to be used. The situation is different,

---

which at any given moment is utilized in cash, and which undergoes sharp seasonal fluctuations. This phenomenon, however, is itself a consequence of the use of bank credit. For a somewhat more detailed discussion of these problems, cf. Lecture IV, of *Prices and Production*.

however, when we are dealing with productive credits granted by the banks to industry — which constitute the most frequent form of increase in the volume of circulating media. These credits are only given when and where their utilization is profitable, or at least appears to be so. Profitability is determined, however, by the ratio of the interest paid on these credits to the profits earned by their use. So long as the amount of credit obtainable at any given rate of interest is limited, competition will ensure that only the most profitable employments are financed out of a given amount of credit. The uses to which the additional money can be put are thus determined by the rate of interest, and the amount which can be said about those uses will therefore depend, in turn, on how much is known about the importance and the effects of interest. Whatever may have been written or thought on this old problem of theoretical economics, it is undeniable that those particular aspects of interest theory which are important for our analysis have so far received less attention and even less recognition than is their due. It is not practicable to work out, within the limits of this essay, the supplementary analysis which seems to me to be necessary in this field; but I should like, at least, to indicate, before I conclude, some angles of approach which appear to have been unduly neglected hitherto. Needless to say, the sections which follow have even less claim than their predecessors to be regarded as comprehensive.

I I

In the economic system of to-day, interest does not exist in the form in which it is presented by pure economic theory. Not only do we find, instead of one uniform rate, a great number of differing rates, but, beyond this, none of the various rates of interest existing is entitled to rank as *the* rate of interest described by static theory, on which all other rates depend, differing only to the extent to which they are affected by special circumstances. The process of interest fixation, which is at the basis of pure theory, never in fact follows the same course in a modern credit economy; for in such an economy the supply of, and the demand for, savings never directly confront each other.

All existing theories of interest, with a few not very successful exceptions, restrict themselves to the explanation of that *imaginary* rate of interest which would result from such an immediate confronting of supply and demand. The fact that the rate of interest which these theories explain is one never found in practice does not mean that they are of no importance, or even that any explanation of the actual rates can afford to ignore them. On the contrary, an adequate explanation of that 'natural rate' is the indispensable starting point for any realization of the conditions necessary to the achievement of equilibrium, and for an understanding of the effects which every rate of interest actually in force exerts on the economic system. It is true that it does not suffice to explain all empirically observed rates since it takes into consideration only one of the factors determining those rates (though that factor is of course, the one which is always operative); but any consideration of ruling interest rates which did not relate its analysis to that of the imaginary interest rate of static theory would hang entirely in the air. For the most part, however, no solution has been found to the wider problem of building up on the basis of the theory of an equilibrium rate of interest, which can be deduced from the credit-less economy, the structure of different rates which can be simultaneously observed in a modern economy. The solution of this particular problem should provide a most valuable contribution to a deeper insight into cyclical fluctuations.

But before we set out to explore on the one hand the difference between the natural rate of interest and the actual rate, and on the other hand that between the various kinds of the latter, we must say something about the importance of changes in the equilibrium rate itself, since some very confused ideas prevail as to the function of the equilibrium rate of interest in a dynamic economy. This is not very surprising since, as we have seen above, an insufficient appreciation of the role of interest is the cause of most misunderstanding in Trade Cycle theory. Perhaps it is not too much to say that the importance which an economist attaches to interest as a regulator of economic development is the best criterion of his theoretical insight. It is therefore all the more regrettable that recent economic literature has been quite fruitless so far as the theory of interest is concerned.* This too is, perhaps, due in part to the fact that the earlier economists, to whom we owe our present knowledge of interest theory, stopped short in their investigations and never came to the point of explaining the actual rates.

III

Under the rubric of *pure interest theory* (by which we understand the explanation of that rate of interest which is not modified by monetary influences, although paid, of course, on capital reckoned in money terms) we shall have to deal briefly with the question of the effect of transitory fluctuations in the natural rate of interest, conditioned by 'real' factors. This question is of great

---

* The best confirmation of this view is given by Mr. G. Heinze, who, in his recent study, *Static or Dynamic Interest Theory* (Leipzig, 1928), comes to the correct conclusion that 'In spite of all the partly justified criticism which was levelled against the interest theory of Böhm-Bawerk, the latter still represents the most logically perfect economic explanation of the phenomenon of interest, and is, moreover the one which comes nearest to the observed facts' (p. 165).

importance, taking as it does a decisive place in some of the best known Trade Cycle theories of our day. In particular Professor Cassel's view (mentioned above, p. 80) that the real cause of cyclical fluctuations lies in an over-estimate of the supply of new capital, is based on the assumption that a temporary fall in the rate of interest conditioned by real causes can bring about over-investment in the same way as a rate of interest artificially lowered by monetary factors. This view, which seems to be supported by a considerable body of experts, has to be judged quite differently according as the changes which elicit fluctuations in the rate of interest originate on the demand or the supply side. Fluctuations caused by changes on the demand side, which Professor Cassel uses as an explanation in his trade cycle theory, certainly cannot be regarded as an adequate explanation of the cycle; for, as Professor Amonn has already pointed out,* this is no reason why enterpreneurs

* *Cassel's System der Theoretischen Nationalökonomie* (Archiv für Sozialwissenschaften und Sozialpolitik, vol. 51, Tübingen, 1924, p. 348 *et seq.*) In order to remain within the scope of our work we have to forgo the very alluring task of criticizing Professor Cassel's argument. Such a criticism would also have to deal with the very

should (assuming an unchanged rate of interest)
expect to obtain more credits in the future than
they can now. However there can be no doubt
that violent fluctuations in savings and the
consequent temporary changes in the equilibrium
rate of interest act similarly to an artificial lowering
of the money rate of interest in causing an extension of capital investments which cannot be
maintained later owing to the diminished supply
of savings.* In this case, therefore, it is permissible
to speak of non-monetary cyclical fluctuations.
This differs, however, from the conception of
cyclical fluctuations employed hitherto, in that
the passage from boom into depression is not a
necessary consequence of the boom itself, but is
conditioned by 'external circumstances'. A downward turn of this sort can occur just as well in a

ingenious theoretical interpretation of this argument by Dr. G. Halm
(Das Zinsproblem am Geld- und Kapitalmarkt, *Jahrbücher für
Nationalökonomie und Statistik*, 3rd series, vol. 70, Jena, 1926, p.
16 *et seq.*) Here we may only point out that in this study Halm is
driven to make use of the old hypothesis that savings accumulate
for a time and are then suddenly utilized 'at the moment when the
real boom begins' (p. 21).

* Cf. Dr. A. Lampe, *Zur Theorie des Sparprozesses und der
Kreditschöpfung* (Jena, 1926, p. 67 *seq.*)

hitherto stationary economy or during a depression as at the end of a boom; and it should therefore be regarded less as an example of a cyclical movement than as a particularly complicated case of the direct process of adjustment to changes in data. In any case, for reasons given above, such an explanation, as compared with an endogenous theory, would only come into play when the latter had proved insufficient to explain a given concrete phenomenon.

But there can be no doubt that such fluctuations in the natural rate, conditioned by changes in the rate of saving activity, present some very important problems in interest theory, the solution of which would be an important aid in estimating the effect of fluctuations conditioned by monetary changes. We have entirely disregarded the circumstances determining the supply of savings and the fluctuations in this supply; and the examination of these is a promising field for future research. It might even be possible to show that fluctuations in saving activity are a necessary concomitant of economic progress, and thus to give a firm basis to the theories which we have mentioned. This is, perhaps, not very probable.

In direct relation to the above problem stands the question of the effects of alterations in the rate of interest on the price system as a whole. An examination of this subject should throw light on the point of view, emphasized by Professor Fetter,* that the height of interest rate, at any given moment expresses itself in the whole structure of price relationships, while every change in that rate must *pari passu* bring about changes in the relation between particular prices and thus in the quantitative relationships of the whole economy.

But here we must content ourselves with drawing attention to the problems arising out of the changes in the natural rate of interest, without contributing further to their solution. We shall only venture a further remark on a question concerning not the consequences but the causes of these changes, since this is important in what follows. This is the question whether

* *Op. cit.*, especially, p. 78. Cf. also, Lecture III, of *Prices and Production*.

the rate of interest at any moment depends on the total amount of capital existing at that moment or only on *the amount of free capital available for new investment*.* We mention this here only in order to emphasize the untenability of the widespread view that the determining factor, on the supply side, is the whole existing stock of capital. If that were so it would hardly be possible to explain any large fluctuations of the rate of interest, since the *relative* changes which the existing capital stock undergoes within brief periods and under normal circumstances is insignificant. A thorough investigation of the interconnections in this field must show that the actual rate of interest depends (apart from the demand for loan capital) only on the supply of newly produced or reproduced capital. The existing stock of fixed capital affects only the demand side, by determining the yields to be expected from new investments. This explains how, in a country which is well equipped with fixed capital,

---

* 'Capital disposable for investment' was the phrase usually employed by the classical writers to distinguish this free capital from the stock of real capital. Cf., e.g., J. S. Mill, *Essays on some unsettled questions of Political Economy*, London, 1844, pp. 113 ff.

the rate of interest can temporarily rise higher than that obtainable in a country which is poorly equipped, provided that there is relatively more free capital available for *new* investment in the latter than in the former. This fact has some significance in connection with the phenomenon of enforced saving with which we shall deal later.

IV

As regards the relationship of the natural or equilibrium rate of interest to the actual rate, it should be noted, in the first place, that even the existence of this distinction is questioned. The objections, however, mainly arise from a misunderstanding which occurred because K. Wicksell, who originated the distinction, made use in his later works of the term 'real rate' (which to my mind is less suitable than 'natural rate') and this expression became more widespread than that which we have used.* The expression 'real rate of interest' is also unsuitable, since it coincides

* Cf. the works of Professor Röpke and Dr. Burchardt, mentioned above; also E. Egner, *Zur Lehre vom Zwangsparen*, 1928, p. 537. Occasionally (*Geldzins und Güterpreise*, p. 111) Wicksell also uses the expression 'normal rate'.

with Professor Fisher's 'real interest',* which, as is well known, denotes the actual rate plus the rate of appreciation or minus the rate of depreciation of money, and is thus in accordance with common usage, which employs the term 'real wages' or 'real income' in the same sense. Unfortunately Wicksell's change in terminology is also linked up with a certain ambiguity in his definition of the 'natural rate'. Having correctly defined it once as 'that rate at which the demand for loan capital just equals the supply of savings't he redefines it, on another occasion, as that rate which would rule 'if there were no money transactions and real capital were lent *in natura*'.‡ If this last definition were correct, Dr. G. Halm§ would be right in raising, against the conception of a 'natural rate', the objection that a uniform rate of interest could develop only in a money economy, so that the whole analysis is

* Cf. especially *Appreciation and Interest* (Publications of the American Economic Association, 3rd series, vol. xi, No. 4, New York, 1896).

† *Vorlesungen*, vol. ii, p. 220.

‡ *Geldzins und Güterpreise*, p. 93.

§ *Op. cit.*, p. 7, footnote.

irrelevant. If Dr. Halm, instead of clinging to this unfortunate formula, had based his reasoning on the correct definition which is also to be found in Wicksell, he would have reached the same conclusion as Professor Adolf Weber—the distinguished head of the school of which he is a member; that is, that the natural rate is a conception 'which is evolved automatically from any clear study of economic interconnections'.* In accordance with this view, Wicksell's conception must be credited with fundamental significance in the study of monetary influences on the economic system; especially if one realizes the practical importance of a money rate of interest depressed below the natural rate by a constantly increasing volume of circulating media. Unfortunately, although **Wick**sell's solution cannot be regarded as adequate at all points, the attention which it has received since he propounded it has borne no relation to its importance. Apart from the works of Professor Mises, mentioned above, the theory has made no progress at all, although many questions concern-

* *Depositenbanken und Spekulationsbanken*, 3rd edit., 1922, p. 171.

ing it still await solution.* This may be due to the fact (on which we have touched already) that the problem had become entangled with that of fluctuations in the general price level. We have already stated our views on this point, (p. 196) and indicated what is necessary for the further development of the theory. Here, we shall try to restate the problem in its correct form, freed from any reference to movements in the price level.

V

Every given structure of production, i.e. every given allocation of goods as between different branches and stages of production, requires a certain definite relationship between the prices of the finished products and those of the means of production. In a state of equilibrium,

* Another attempt to develop Wicksell's theory — of which I have learnt only since the above was written — was made, at roughly the time when Mises' work was published, by Prof. M. Fanno of Padua in a work entitled *Le banche e il mercato monetario*, Rome 1912. An abridged restatement of Prof. Fanno's theory will shortly appear, in German, in a volume of essays on monetary theory by a number of Dutch, Italian and Swedish authors, edited by the author of the present essay.

the difference necessarily existing between these two sets of prices must correspond to the rate of interest, and at this rate, just as much must be saved from current consumption and made available for investment as is necessary for the maintenance of that structure of production. The latter condition necessarily follows from the fulfilment of the former, since the prices paid for the means of production, plus interest, can only correspond to the prices of the resulting products when, at the given prices and rate of interest, the supply of producers' goods is exactly adequate to maintain production on the existing scale. The price margins between means of production and products, therefore, can only remain constant and in correspondence with the rate of interest so long as the proportion of current income, which at the given rate of interest is not consumed but reinvested in production, remains exactly equal to the necessary capital required to carry on production. Every change in this proportion must begin by impairing the correspondence of price margins and the interest rate; for it influences both in opposite directions, and so leads to further shifts in the whole structure of production, representing an adjustment to altered price-relationships. These resulting changes in the structure of production will not always be the same; they will vary according to whether the change in the proportions of the social income going respectively to consumption goods and investment goods corresponds to real changes in the decisions of individuals as to spending and saving, or whether it was brought about artificially, without any corresponding changes in individual saving activity.

Apart from individual saving activity (which includes, of course the savings of corporations, of the State and of other bodies entitled to raise compulsory contributions) the proportions between consumption and capital creation can only change as a result of alterations in the effective quantity of money.* When changes in the division of the total social dividend, in favour of capital creation, result from changes in the saving activity of individuals, they are self-perpetuating. This

* Very instructive investigations of the problems considered here were carried out by A. Lampe: *Zur Theorie des Sparprozesses und der Kreditschöpfung*, Jena, 1926.

is not true of such variations between 'consumption and accumulation' (if we may use for once the terminology of Marxian literature) as are due to additional credits granted to the entrepreneurs; these can be assumed to persist only so long as the proportion is kept artificially high by a progressively increasing rate of credit creation. Such an injection of money into circulation acts only temporarily — *until the additional money becomes income. At that moment, the proportion of capital creation must relapse to the level of voluntary saving activity,* unless *new* credits are granted bearing the same relation to the new total of money incomes as the first injection bore to the former total.*

* The argument presented in the text (and put in this form for brevity's sake) is imperfect in two respects. Firstly, the flow of voluntary saving can itself vary as a result of a single change in the proportion of capital formation. This factor, however, is unlikely to become important enough for its omission to affect the exposition given in the text. Secondly, the way in which the additional money, which was given in the first instance to entrepreneurs and used by them to lengthen the period of production, will always swell incomes in the long run, needs further elaboration. As a general proposition, however, it is obvious that whoever uses the additional credits to make additional investment goods can do so only by employing additional factors of production; and therefore, since there is in our case no compensating decrease in the demand for factors elsewhere, the total incomes of the factors must increase.

It is clear that such a process of progressive increase in the supply of money cannot be maintained under our existing credit system, especially since, as it proceeds, more extensive use will be made of cash. On the other hand, a mere cessation of further increases — not, therefore, a reversal of credit policy, towards deflation — is sufficient to bring back the proportion of total income available for capital formation to the extent of voluntary savings.

The differences in the effects of these two kinds of variation between consumption and capital formation manifest themselves first of all on the price system, and thus on the natural or equilibrium rate of interest. The first effect of *a diminution of the rate on loans arising from increased saving activity* — so long as the structure of production remains unchanged — is to bring that rate below the margin between the prices of means of production and of products. The increased saving activity, however, must soon cause on the one hand a falling off in the demand for consumption goods, and hence a tendency for their prices to fall (a tendency which may merely find expression in decreasing sales at existing prices) and, on the other hand, an increase in the demand for investment goods and thus a rise in their prices. The extension of production will have a further depressing effect on the prices of consumption goods, as the new products come on the market, until, finally, the difference between the respective prices has shrunk to a magnitude corresponding to the new, lower, interest rate. If, however, the fall in the rate of interest is due to an *increase in the circulating media*, it can never lead to a corresponding diminution in the price margin, or to a readjustment of the two sets of prices to the level of an equilibrium rate of interest which will endure. In this case, moreover, the increased demand for investment goods will bring about a net increase in the demand for consumption goods; and therefore the price margin cannot be narrowed more than is permitted by the time-lag in the rise of consumption goods prices — a lag existing only as long as the process of inflation continues. As soon as the cessation of credit inflation puts a stop to the rise in the prices of investment goods, the difference between these and the prices of consumption goods will increase again, not only to its previous level but beyond, since, in the course of inflation, the structure of production has been so shifted that in comparison with the division of the social income between expenditure and saving the supply of consumption goods will be relatively less, and that of production goods relatively greater, than before the inflation began.*

V I

There have recently been increasingly frequent objections to this account of the effects of an increased volume of currency, and the artificial lowering of interest rates conditioned by it, on the grounds that it disregards certain supposedly beneficial effects which are closely connected with this phenomenon. What the objectors have in mind is the phenomenon of so-called 'forced saving' which has received great attention in recent literature.† This phenomenon, we are

* Cf. my article on *The 'Paradox' of Saving*, 'Economica,' No. 32, p. 160.

† Besides Leon Walras – the originator of this theory (Cf. his *Etudes d'économie politique appliquée* 1898, pp. 348–356),

to understand, consists in an increase in capital creation at the cost of consumption, through the granting of additional credit, *without* voluntary action on the part of the individuals who forgo consumption, and without their deriving any immediate benefit. According to the usual presentation of the theory of forced saving, this occurs through a fall in the general value of money, which diminishes the consumers' purchasing power; the volume of goods thus freed can be used by the producers who obtained additional credits. We must, however, raise the same objection to this theory which we raised against the usual account of the effects of an artificial lowering of the money rate of interest, i.e. that, in principle, forced saving takes place whenever the volume of money is increased, and does not need to

Wicksell and the well-known works of Professors Mises and Schumpeter, one must mention the recent works of Professor Röpke, Dr. Egner, and Dr. Neisser; and in Anglo-Saxon literature, Mr. D. H. Robertson's *Banking Policy and the Price Level* (London, 1926). As I have pointed out, however, in Lecture I of *Prices and Production* and – at somewhat greater length – in *A Note on the Development of the Theory of Forced Saving*, in the *Quarterly Journal of Economics*, November, 1932, he concept of 'forced saving' was already known to J. Bentham, H. Thornton, T. R. Malthus and a number of other writers in the early 19th century, down to J. S. Mill.

manifest itself in changes in the value of money.*

The 'depreciation' of money in the hands of the consumer can be, and frequently will be, only relative, in the sense that those diminutions in price which would otherwise have occurred are prevented from occurring. Even this causes a part of the social dividend to be distributed to individuals who have not acquired legitimate claim to it through previous services, nor taken them over from others legitimately entitled to them. It is thus taken away from this part of the community against its will. After what has been said above, this process needs no further illumination.

Nor do we need to adduce further proof that every grant of additional credit induces 'forced saving' — even if we have avoided using this rather unfortunate expression in the course of our argument. There is only one further point — the effect of this artificially induced capital accumulation — on which a few remarks should be added. It has

* Cf. D. H. Robertson, *Money*, 2nd edit., p. 99; and A. C. Pigou, *Industrial Fluctuations*, 2nd edit., 1929, pp. 251–257.

often been argued that the forced saving arising from an artificially lowered interest rate would improve the capital supply of the economy to such an extent that the natural rate of interest would have to fall finally to the level of the money rate of interest, and thus a new state of equilibrium would be created — that is, the crisis could be avoided altogether. This view is closely connected with the thesis, which we have already rejected, that the level of the natural rate of interest depends directly upon the whole existing stock of real capital. Forced saving increases only the existing stock of real capital goods, but not necessarily the current supply of free capital disposable for investment — that portion of total income which is not consumed but used as a provision for the upkeep and depreciation of fixed plant. But any addition to the supply of free capital available for new investment or reinvestment must come from those of the investments induced by forced savings which already yield a return; a return large enough to leave over, after providing for supplementary costs connected with the new means of production, a surplus for depreciation and for interest payments on the capital. If the capital supply from this source is to lower the natural rate of interest, it must not, of course, be offset by a diminution elsewhere — resulting from the decline of other undertakings confronted with the reinforced competition of those newly supplied with capital.

The assumption that an artificial increase of fixed capital (i.e. one caused by additional credits) tends to diminish the natural rate of interest in the same way as one effected through voluntary savings activity presupposes, therefore, that the new capital must be incorporated into the economic system in such a way that the prices of the products imputed to it shall cover interest and depreciation. Now a given stock of capital goods is not a factor which will maintain and renew itself automatically, irrespective of whether it is in accordance with the current supply of savings or not. The fact that investments have been undertaken which cannot be 'undone' offers no guarantee whatever that this is the case. Whether capital can be created beyond the limits set by voluntary saving depends — and this is just as true for its renewal as for the creation of new plant — on whether the process of credit creation continues in a steadily increasing ratio. If the new processes of production are to be completed, and if those already in existence are to continue in employment, it is essential that additional credits should be continually injected at a rate which increases fast enough to keep ahead, by a constant proportion, of the expanding purchasing power of the consumer. If a new process of roundabout production can be completed while these conditions still hold good, it can contribute temporarily to a lowering of the natural rate of interest; but this provides no final solution of the difficulty.

For, eventually, a moment must inevitably arrive when the banks are unable any longer to keep up the rate of inflation required, and at that moment there must always be some processes of production, newly undertaken and not yet completed,* which were only ventured because

* The existence of new long processes, which have not yet been completed, is not a necessary condition in order that the relative increase in the demand for consumers' goods may lead to the abandonment of such processes and, therefore, to the destruction of part of the capital employed there; but it is the case which will always be given in

the rate of interest was kept artificially low. It does not follow, of course, that these processes in particular will be left unfinished because of the subsequent rise in that rate; on the other hand, their existence does cause the rate of interest to be higher than it would be in their absence, when capital would be required only by processes made possible by voluntary saving without any competing demand arising from processes which were only enabled to start by 'forced saving.' The capital invested in new and not yet completed processes of production will thus merely intensify the demand for further supplies by calling for the capital necessary to complete them — an effect which will be the more pronounced the greater the

practice and where this effect is most easily seen. In this connection it should, however, be noted that the introduction of a longer round-about process of production will, in almost all cases, affect not only a single enterprise but a series of enterprises representing successive stages of production. Even a completed plant may, in this sense, represent part of an incomplete process — if the capital is lacking which would have to be invested in the machines or other capital goods to be produced by this plant. Plant equipped to satisfy a demand for machinery which cannot be permanently maintained is, in this sense, part of a roundabout process which cannot be continued. For a fuller description, see *Prices and Production*, Lecture III and, especially, my article, *Kapitalaufzehrung* in the Weltwirtschaftliches Archiv, July 1932.

ratio of capital invested to capital still required. It may therefore quite easily come about that, in order to complete these newly initiated processes, capital may be diverted from the maintenance of complete and old-established undertakings, so that new plant is put into operation and old plant closed down, although the latter would have been kept up, and the former never put in hand, if it had been a question of building up the whole capital equipment of the economy from the start. This does not merely mean that the total return comes to less than it otherwise would; it also means, primarily, that production is forced into channels to which it will only keep for as long as the new and spuriously produced stock of fixed capital can remain in use. The value of capital invested in processes which can be continued, and, still more, that in processes where continuance is impracticable, will shrink rapidly in value — this shrinkage being accompanied by the phenomena of a crisis. Thus on purely technical grounds it will become uneconomic to maintain them. It should be particularly remarked that, from the point of view of the fate of individual enterprises, capital invested in fixed plant, but raised by borrowing, is of precisely the same importance as working capital, i.e. the loss of value does not merely necessitate writing down, it generally makes it impossible to carry on at all.

The cause of this development is, evidently, that an unwarranted accumulation of capital has been taking place; though people may regard it (under the alluring name of 'forced saving') as a thoroughly desirable phenomenon. After what has been said above *it is probably more proper to regard forced saving as the cause of economic crises than to expect it to restore a balanced structure of production.*

V I I

There remains one problem of interest theory, in the wider sense of the word, which we need to examine more closely than we have yet done — in order to exhibit a problem of first-class importance to the progress of Trade Cycle theory. This is the problem of the varying height and independent movements of rates of interest ruling at the same place and at the same time. We are not thinking, of course, of differences conditioned either by the unequal standing of borrowers or by the fact that under the name of interest payments are also made for the services or costs connected with the granting of credit. We are interested only in the problem of variations arising *within* the pure or net rate of interest, as they can be observed between credits of varying duration — the problem usually known in economic literature as the problem of interest rates, in the *money*, and in the *capital* (investment) market, respectively.

In this respect we may repeat what we have already said at the beginning of this chapter — that the theoretical investigations of interest have been broken off at far too early a stage to afford much understanding of the rates actually ruling at any given moment. It is very remarkable that none of the great theorists to whom we owe our insight into the fundamental factors determining the equilibrium rate of interest made the slightest attempt to explain these differences between interest rates. Systematic investigation of this problem came much later and then characteristically the investigation related chiefly to the question of the 'external order of the capital or money market'; and it is only recently that Dr. G. Halm* has treated the simultaneous existence of varying interest rates 'as a problem of interest theory'. Although Dr. Halm deserves full credit for the undeniable service he has rendered in putting the problem in the proper form for discussion, his attempt at solution can hardly be regarded as fully successful. Thus we still stand

---

* 'Das Zinsproblem am Geld und Kapitalmarkt' *Jahrbücher für Nationalökonomie und Statistik*, 3rd series, No. 125, vol. 70, Jena 1926. Of the comprehensive bibliography given by Halm, the following, together with some more recent additions, are worth mention: A. Spiethoff: (1) *Die äussere Ordnung des Kapital und Geldmarktes;* (2) *Das Verhältnis von Kapital, Geld und Güterwelt;* (3) *Der Kapitalmangel in seinem Verhältnis zur Güterwelt;* all in Schmloler's *Jahrbuch*, vol. 33 (München, 1909). Also, by the same author: *Der Begriff des Kapital und Geldmarktes*, Schmoller's *Jahrbuch*, vol. 44, 1920 H. von Beckerath *Kapital und Geldmarkt* (Jena 1916).

Professor Schumpeter's Dr. Neisser's and Professor Fetter's works already mentioned; A. Hahn: *Zur Theorie des Geldmarktes* (Archiv für Sozialwissenschaften und Sozialpolitik, vol. 51, Tübingen, 1924). Karin Kock: *A Study of Interest Rates*, Stockholm Economic Studies, No. 1, London, 1929.

W. W. Riefler, *Money Rates and Markets in the United States* (New York and London, 1930).

The problems arising out of empirical research are well summarized by O. Donner and A. Hanau, 'Untersunchung zur Frage der Marktzusammenhänge' (*Vierteljahrshefte zur Konjunkturforschung*, 3rd year, No. 3 A, Institut für Konjunkturforschung, Berlin 1928), an investigation which is a model of its kind.

at the beginning of a crucially important development of a special theory cf money rates of interest.

The clearing up of these interconnections is of primary importance to Trade Cycle theory, since the discrepancies between the expected yields of existing means of production and the actual yield obtainable from the available liquid capital must necessarily arise in the course of the cycle. Given a sufficient insight into the influences determining the yields of both types of investment, the simultaneous changes in the height of both kinds of interest rates should afford extraordinarily valuable material for the diagnosis of any actual situation, and thus the growth of this part of interest theory would provide an important basis for the development of empirical research and forecasting. A particularly promising approach might consist in an examination of the question from the point of view of an equalization of the time-differences between the rates of interest which would prevail if the whole supply of capital, at any time, had to be invested for a longer period. Such an equalization would be brought about by a kind of *arbitrage* for which, naturally, only money lent at call or at short notice could be considered.

In this field, too, the extension of equilibrium analysis to successively occurring phenomena, which I have attempted in another work,* may prove fruitful. At any rate, an explanation of this arbitrage could also explain why the rates on short-term credits can be temporarily lower, or on the other hand higher, than the long-term rate, since both borrower and lender would find such an arbitrage to their advantage. This view cannot be refuted by the objection that the rates on short-term credits not only change earlier but also change to a greater degree than those in the capital market; for it may be economically entirely justifiable to pay higher rates or obtain lower ones, for a short term, than one expects for a long term, since the expectation of getting better terms at a later period, under more favourable conditions, may compensate for the relative disadvantages suffered in the short run.

* Cf. 'Das intertemporale Gleichgewichtssystem der Preise und die Bewegungen des Geldwertes' – already quoted.

VIII

Finally, we should like to point out quite briefly certain tasks in the field of statistical research which according to our theoretical analysis seem likely to be particularly fruitful. In connection with the last question dealt with, we should draw attention to the statistics of the money market, which are still, unfortunately, in a very elementary stage, partly for technical reasons but mainly because of difficulties of interpretation. These latter arise largely from the fact that the statistical determination of the absolute height of the interest rate, or even of its movements, discloses almost nothing as to its bearing on the economic system.* The same rate of interest which at one moment may be too low in relation to the whole economic situation may be too high at the next, or vice versa. Misunderstandings on this point may be responsible for certain erroneous views,

* The statistical determination of nominal changes in the interest rate is also rendered very difficult by the fact that changes can take place in the form of changes in stipulations as to the quality of the bills discounted at a given rate, and so on. The same rate may be merely applied to a better class of borrowers, or the same borrowers may be required to pay a higher rate.

concerning the alleged insignificance of the height of interest rates, which are often held by statistical economists. The innumerable attempts to minimize the significance of interest rates by means of statistical investigations, which abound in the United States* (where they do not even shrink from such absurdities as an attempt to find an explanation (!) of interest by way of statistical investigation) would be impossible but for the complete confusion persisting as to the limits of statistical research. Here again we have to repeat what was asserted at the beginning of this book: statistics can never prove or disprove a theoretical explanation, they can only present problems or offer fields for theoretical research.

For precisely this reason — viz. that the absolute height of interest rates tells us nothing of their significance — an examination of the extent and regularity of *shifts* between various interest rates offers a promising field for statistical technique. An interesting first attempt in this direction

* Cf. e.g. Snyder, 'The Influence of the Interest Rate on the Business Cycle, *American Economic Review*, vol. xv, December 1925; reprinted in *Business Cycles and Business Measurements* (New York, 1927).

is the famous 'Three Market Barometer' of the Harvard Economic Service, which uses the trend of the long-term interest rate as a base-line in plotting the curve of the money market rates. Such an empirical consideration of the differences between interest rates does not, of course, exhaust the lines of approach which a complete theoretical explanation of these rates might indicate as suitable for empirical research. The fact that theoretical research itself can be stimulated and awakened to new problems to an important degree from the application of our sketchy knowledge to statistical investigations is amply demonstrated by the investigations of Donner and Hanau, which we have already mentioned.

It is in the statistics of private banking, however, that the heaviest task presents itself. In Europe we are still worse supplied with these than with those of the money market proper. In the United States, on the other hand, some pioneer work has been done in this field,* since the ample

* Cf. first of all A. A. Young, 'An Analysis of Bank Statistics for the United States' (reprinted from *The Review of Economic Statistics*, October 1924, January and April 1925, and July 1927) (Cambridge 1928); H. Working, 'Prices and the Quantity of the Circulating Medium,

statistical material available there provided is itself a sufficient incentive for such investigations. In Europe the lack of any kind of material makes even a first step in this direction impossible.

In many respects the most remarkable of these enquiries are those of Mr. Holbrook Working. Using the data concerning the state of deposits in the 'National Banks', which are available for many years past and at intervals of only a few months, he succeeds in establishing a far-reaching parallelism between the movements of deposits and the fluctuations of the wholesale price-level. Like most theoretical investigations in the same field, however, his results are distorted by the superficial assumption that monetary influences can only manifest themselves in movements of the price

1890–1921' (*The Quarterly Journal of Economics*, vol. **xxxvii**, Cambridge, 1923) and 'Bank Deposits as a Forecaster of the General Wholesale Price Level' (*The Review of Economic Statistics*, Cambridge, Mass., 1926) of the same author, C. Snyder, 'Deposits Activity as a Measure of Business Activity' (*Review of Economic Statistics*, Cambridge, Mass., 1924, reprinted in *Business Cycles and Business Measurements*. New York, 1927), W. M. Persons, 'Cyclical Fluctuations of the Ratio of Bank Loans to Deposits (*Review of Economic Statistics*, Cambridge, Mass., 1924). L. A. Hahn, 'Zur Frage des volkswirtschaftlichen Erkenntnisinhaltes der Bankbilanzziffern' (*Vierteljahrshefte zur Konjunkturforschung*, 1, Jahrgang, Erganzungsheft 4, Berlin, 1927).

level, while those changes in the volume of bank credits which are just sufficient to prevent changes in the price level are supposed, on this assumption, to exercise no active influence on the Trade Cycle. It should be mentioned — as having particular bearing upon the views developed in this essay — that, according to Mr. Working's calculations, before the War a yearly increase in deposits of more than 5 per cent would have been necessary in order to keep the price-level steady; that is to say, additional credits would have had to be created to an extent which must have caused considerable changes in the structure of production.

If the results of our theoretical analysis were to be subjected to statistical investigation, it is not the connection between changes in the volume of bank credit and movements in the price level which would have to be explored. Investigation would have to start on the one hand from alterations in the rate of increase and decrease in the volume and turnover of bank deposits and, on the other, from the extent of production in those industries which as a rule expand excessively as a result of credit injection.* Every increase in the circulating media brings about the same effect, so long as each *stands in the same proportion* to the existing volume; and only an increase in this proportion makes possible a further increase in investment activity. On the other hand, every diminution of the *rate of increase* in itself causes some portion of existing investment, made possible through credit creation, to become unprofitable. It follows that a curve exhibiting the monetary influences on the course of the cycle ought to show, not the movements in the total volume of circulating media, but the alteration in the rate of change of this volume.† Every up-turn of this curve would show that an artificial lowering of the money rate of interest or, if the curve was already rising, a further lowering of the money rates, was making possible additional investments

* Cf. the instructive graphs given by Harold L. Reed in his *Federal Reserve Policy* 1921–1930 (New York and London 1930), pp. 181 *et seq.*

† Mathematically speaking, the question is one of the graphical presentation, in place of the curve showing the original movements at any moment, of the first differential of this function. On the subject of this method, which has been frequently used of late, cf. I. Fisher, *The Business Cycle Largely a 'Dance of the Dollar'* (Quarterly Publication of the American Statistical Association. December, 1923).

for which voluntary savings would not suffice; and every down-turn would show that current credit-creation was no longer sufficient to ensure the continuance of all the enterprises which it originally called into existence. It would be of great interest to correlate this presentation of the influence causing an excessive production of capital goods with actual changes in the production of these goods, on the basis of available data.

The possible contributions of banking statistics to Trade Cycle research are by no means exhausted by the chance they offer of observing the immediate connection between the granting of credit and the movements of production, though these may some day constitute the most important basis of business forecasting. No less important would be an investigation into the volume, at any given moment, of those factors which determine credit expansion, under the other headings of bank balance sheets, and, in particular, an examination of the relation between the total amount of earning assets and the current accounts, the relation between these and the cash-circulation, and so on. Such an investigation, if it were not merely to exhibit their movements in time but also to analyse the deeper connections between them, and most especially if it were to clear up the relationship between interest rates, profits, and the liquidity of the banks, would further our insight into the factors determining credit expansion as well as our knowledge of their limits, and thus make it possible to forecast movements in the factors determining the total development of the economic situation.

It is very unfortunate that such inquiries, especially on the continent of Europe, are almost impossible owing to the lack of necessary data in the form of returns showing the state of the banks, and published at short intervals; in so far as they are possible at all it is only in a few countries and for a very short period. As soon as it is realized that, owing to the existence of banks, the equilibrating forces of the economic system cannot bring about that automatic adjustment of all its branches to the actual situation, which is described by classical economic theory, it is justifiable even from a liberal point of view that the banks should be subjected to degrees of publicity as to the state of their business which is not necessary in the case of other undertakings; and this would by no means imply a violation of the principle of business secrecy, since it would be quite sufficient for this purpose if the authorities were to adopt the United States' plan of publishing summary returns for all banks at frequent intervals. Our reflections thus yield the conclusion that an alleviation of cyclical fluctuations should be expected pre-eminently from a greater publicity among business enterprises, and particularly among the banks. The example of the United States, which is far ahead in this respect in all the branches of its economic system, will not only silence in time the objections raised against such publicity, but sooner or later will force us to follow in their path.

INDEX OF AUTHORS CITED

INDEX OF AUTHORS CITED

INDEX

Löwe, A., 27, 29, 33, 42, 53, 93, 94, 105, 121, 122, 127, 141, 144, 184, 188

MACLEOD, H. D., 110, 153
Marshall, A., 110, 139
Menger, C., 117
Miksch, L., 42
Mill, James, 42
Mill, J. S., 208, 219
Miller, A. C., 22
Mises, L., 47, 48, 110, 111, 116, 117, 118, 119, 124, 128, 133, 144, 145, 150, 153, 181, 211, 219
Mitchell, W. C., 53, 58, 63, 97, 129
Morgenstern, O., 36, 83, 192

NEISSER, H., 145, 153, 163, 164, 176, 219, 228
Nicholson, J. S., 110

PENNINGTON, J., 153
Persons, W. M., 38, 53, 234
Phillips, C. O., 153, 154, 161, 172
Pigou, A. C., 31, 83, 191, 220

REED, H.L., 236
Reisch, R., 153, 155, 164, 165
Ricardo, D., 110
Riefler, W. W., 228

Robertson, D. H., 62, 63, 64, 115, 219, 220
Rodkey, R. G., 153
Röpke, W., 46, 111, 181, 188, 209, 219

SAY, J.B., 42, 101
Schlesinger, K., 139, 164
Schumpeter, J., 57, 60, 97, 163, 168, 183, 219, 228.
Sidgwick, H., 110
Snyder, C., 232, 234
Spiethoff, A., 41, 79, 80, 89, 90, 105, 133, 134, 228
Strigl, R., 181
Stucken, R., 115

THORNTON, H., 109, 152, 219
Timoshenko, V. P., 168
Tooke, T., 153
Torrens, R., 153

WALRAS, L., 218
Weber, A., 153, 211
Wicksell, K., 34, 47, 110, 111, 113ff, 128, 133, 134, 145, 146, 148, 153, 178, 209, 210, 211, 212, 219
Wieser, F., 108
Withers, H., 153, 154
Working, H., 233, 234, 235

YOUNG, A. A., 233